CIVIL WAR LEGACY
IN THE SHENANDOAH

CIVIL WAR LEGACY
IN THE SHENANDOAH

Remembrance, Reunion & Reconciliation

Jonathan A. Noyalas

THE
History
PRESS

Published by The History Press
Charleston, SC 29403
www.historypress.net

Copyright © 2015 by Jonathan A. Noyalas
All rights reserved

First published 2015

ISBN 978.1.5402.1318.1

Library of Congress Control Number: 2015932374

This book is dedicated to the loving memory of my two grandfathers, John A. Noyalas and Robert F. Klementovicz, members of the greatest generation who were willing to sacrifice all during World War II to defend the "Four Freedoms." May they both enjoy eternal peace.

CONTENTS

PREFACE

O n the eve of the Civil War centennial, poet and writer Walker Percy hoped that a century after the Civil War's end, historians would move away from traditional studies of campaigns and battles and examine the "history of the shifting attitudes toward the War" since its conclusion.[1] While Percy's dream for historians to grapple with the complex issues of Civil War memory did not come true during the centennial, historians such as David Blight, Stuart McConnell, Edward Lilenthal, Joan Waugh and Caroline Janney have produced works in the recent past that have answered Percy's call.[2] Despite the splendid scholarship of these historians, much work still remains. In particular, much needs to be done to garner a better understanding of how various localities that experienced war on an incessant basis coped with the Civil War's immediate aftermath, made sense of the conflict, came to terms with its results and opened up to the idea of some level of reconciliation. As part of the quest to gain an understanding of the "shifting attitudes toward the War," this book focuses on a region that experienced the conflict on a scale and with a frequency perhaps unparalleled during four years of bloody civil war—Virginia's Shenandoah Valley.

Throughout the conflict, the Shenandoah Valley became a thoroughfare for both armies, served as an avenue of invasion into the North and a source of provender for Confederate forces operating in the Old Dominion and became a point from which Union forces blocked Confederate attempts to move against Washington, D.C. The Shenandoah Valley's strategic importance resulted in numerous raids, occupations, skirmishes and battles—325 according to one National Park Service study.[3] While there has been significant scholarship on military operations during the Civil War in the Shenandoah Valley and several studies of the various campaigns' impact on the region's civilian population, no study has yet been produced that examines how the region's inhabitants—an overwhelming majority of whom supported the Confederacy—reacted to Confederate defeat, chronicles their immediate postwar thoughts about the Civil War or traces the evolution of sentiment from hatred to a level of forgiveness in the half century after the conflict. Furthermore, no examination has yet been written that tracks the activities of Union veterans to memorialize their efforts in the Shenandoah Valley and engage in activities with former Confederates aimed at healing the Civil War's deep wounds.

This study attempts to bring to light, for the first time ever, a history that tracks postwar attitudes of the Shenandoah Valley's inhabitants, namely former Confederates, and how the efforts of Union veterans in the region prompted many former Confederates to forgive their old foes. Despite the willingness of many of the region's former Confederates to forgive their former enemies, this study will show that forgiveness never equated to abandoning their Confederate past or halted efforts of Confederate veterans to pass down their heritage to future generations. Additionally, this study examines how, despite the desire of many Confederates to forgive, some maintained their hatred for Union veterans until the grave. The animosity that some Confederate veterans nursed until death, as this book will also argue, was directed not exclusively at Union veterans but also toward Confederate veterans who embraced the ideas of reconciliation and participated in activities intended to ameliorate the relationships between former foes.

This book's genesis began around a decade ago when Shenandoah University, my undergraduate alma mater, invited me to speak about the Civil War's meaning at a conference in Winchester, Virginia, about the Civil War's legacy that included presentations by Gary Gallagher, Joan Waugh, Caroline Janney, Allen Guelzo, John Hennessy and David Blight. During research for that presentation, I uncovered information about the Sheridan's Veterans' Association (SVA), an organization that is at this book's epicenter—a very fortunate occurrence, for it had never before been examined by anyone. Research into the SVA's activities shed light on other dimensions of the Shenandoah Valley's postwar saga of reunion, remembrance and reconciliation—previously ignored by historians—a discovery that placed me on a ten-year research path gathering materials to construct this volume.

PREFACE

During that period of research and writing, I had opportunities to test out portions of this book at a number of professional conferences, including the Virginia Forum, Gettysburg College's Future of Civil War History Conference, Shenandoah University's McCormick Civil War Institute and the annual Civil War symposium in Springfield, Ohio. Interactions with audience members and panelists at those conferences—individuals such as David Blight, John Hennessy, Karen Cox, Kevin Levin, Leonard Lanier and John Marszalek—have sharpened my focus. Whether these aforementioned individuals are cognizant of this or not, they have all shaped my thinking on the very complex issue of the campaign for postwar reconciliation in the Shenandoah Valley.

In addition to that group of esteemed historians with whom I have had the fortune to share the podium over the years, others played a significant role in this rather tremendous undertaking. The people I recognize here have in some way contributed to this volume but are in no way at fault for any of its errors: Dr. Brandon H. Beck, my undergraduate mentor at Shenandoah University and friend who, throughout this project, encouraged me and offered his own keen historical insight on issues related to historical memory, one shaped not only by his tremendous knowledge of Civil War history but also global history; Walter Blenderman, who offered assistance with Reverend Benjamin F. Whittemore; Nan Card at the Rutherford B. Hayes Presidential Center in Fremont, Ohio, who has been a strong advocate of my work for years and is always willing to assist me in acquiring material from that repository's splendid archives; Rebecca Ebert, archivist of the Stewart Bell Jr. Archives, Handley Regional Library in Winchester, for all her efforts; Chaz W. Evans-Haywood, clerk of the court for Rockingham County, Virginia, who provided access to the splendid image of Colonel D.H. Lee Martz that appears in this book; Penny Imeson, executive director of the Harrisonburg-Rockingham Historical Society in Dayton, Virginia, who offered assistance with research into Confederate veteran John Paul and was extremely gracious in sharing items from the museum's collections; Troy Marshall, executive director of the Virginia Museum of the Civil War and New Market Battlefield State Historical Park, for graciously providing me with information about the dedication of the Fifty-fourth Pennsylvania monument at New Market; Seymour Paul, a descendant and master of all things related to Judge John Paul, who willingly shared his extensive research and collections; Nicholas P. Picerno, a great friend and undisputed expert on the glorious Twenty-ninth Maine Infantry who always opens up his home and collections for my research and whose assistance and friendship is valued more than he can ever know; Christopher Jordan of Kabletown, West Virginia, the undeniable expert on the Fourteenth New Hampshire Infantry, for sharing items from his collection; my dear friend and splendid Shenandoah Valley historian Nancy Sorrells, who willingly shared information with me about the legacy of the Burning in Augusta County; Philip Way, commander of the Colonel D.H. Lee Martz Sons of Confederate Veterans Camp in Harrisonburg, Virginia, who graciously offered assistance when it came to issues related to Colonel Martz; and Karen Wisecarver, the interlibrary loan specialist at my institution, Lord Fairfax Community College, who always goes above and beyond the call of duty in acquiring materials from other institutions. Last, but certainly not least, I would like to thank the two most important people in my life, whom I love more than words could ever express and who are my inspiration: my wonderful son, Alexander, his daddy's best buddy, who always loves exploring Civil War battlefields, and my soul mate, best friend and love of my life, Brandy, a fine historian and educator. Without Brandy's patience, love, keen editorial eye and encouragement, this book would have never reached completion. A husband could never ask for a better wife.

INTRODUCTION

In the Civil War's aftermath, Confederate veterans who called the Shenandoah Valley home returned to their families, farms and businesses. Incessant fighting and occupations by the armies of blue and gray had taken a toll on the region's inhabitants, landscape and economy. Confederate veterans who now reentered their role as civilians had much to do to rebuild the region, but perhaps more important than reconstructing barns and mills or replanting fields, the region's residents, particularly those who supported the Confederacy during the conflict, had to open up to the idea of coming to terms with the war's result and take an active part in healing the Civil War's wounds. The Shenandoah Valley's former Confederates had to, in the words of author Julia Davis, "learn to forget, to forget the terror and glory, the lost vain hopes, and to forget the bitterness."[4]

Among all of the tasks former Confederates had to deal with in the Civil War's aftermath, "learning to forget the bitterness" proved perhaps the most difficult. In the Civil War's immediate wake, most former Confederates simply could not open themselves to the idea of any form of reconciliation with their Union counterparts. The conflict had resulted in Confederate defeat, the dissolution of the institution of slavery (thus placing African Americans, at least constitutionally, on an equal plane with whites) and such destruction that some families stood at the precipice of economic disaster, the pressures and stresses of which forced some into an early grave.[5]

While former Confederates in the Shenandoah Valley tried to learn to forget the bitterness, their Union counterparts desired to honor their fallen

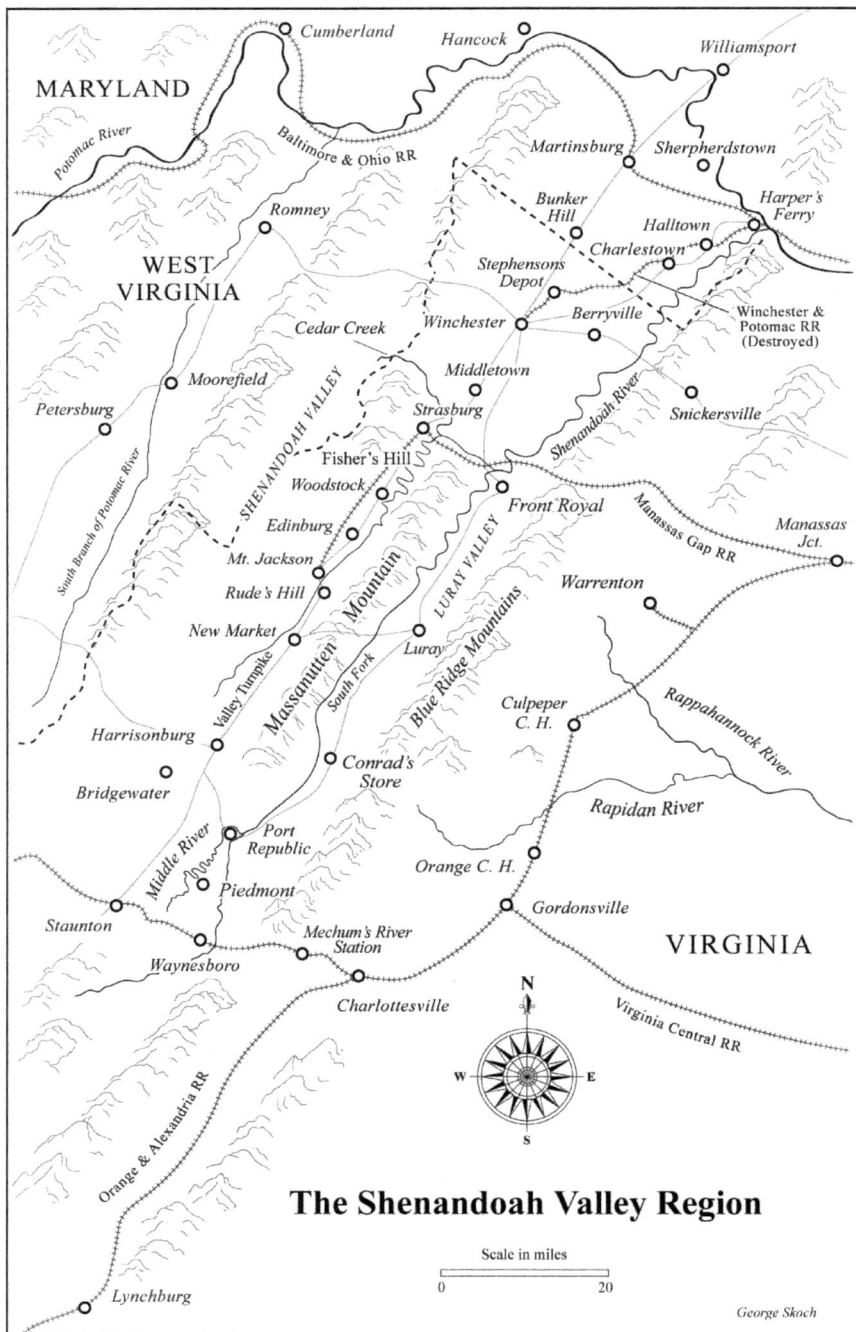

Map of the Shenandoah Valley. *Prepared by George Skoch.*

comrades on the Shenandoah Valley's battlefields. These landscapes were, as one author poignantly observed, places long revered by those in the South and also "sacred now to the North" as "out of their courage and their pain... rose a united nation...[of] one people."[6]

When tensions did eventually ease due to the end of military Reconstruction in the 1870s, population recovery, political transformations and the stabilization of the Shenandoah Valley's economy by the early 1880s, many of the region's former Confederates opened to the idea of welcoming Union veterans. However, former Confederates refused to welcome them as veterans of a conquering army but rather as men with whom they had shared experiences of hardship and sacrifice in camp, on the march and on the battlefield.

Once former Confederates opened themselves to the idea of engaging with Union veterans in activities of postwar reconciliation, sentiments of forgiveness and national healing became more widespread among Confederate veterans. However, what did not become prevalent, especially as Confederate veterans confronted the reality of their mortality, were Confederate veterans willing to abandon their Confederate past, including any admission that secession or slavery was wrong. Likewise, Union veterans who interacted with former Confederates in the Shenandoah Valley, although at first refusing to address any of the conflict's divisive issues—such as secession's constitutionality or slavery's central role in the rupture between North and South—had no qualms about defending the Union cause or their conduct in such actions as destroying civilian property in the valley.[7]

Understanding the evolution of sentiment in the Civil War's immediate wake, the dichotomy of veterans willing to forgive their foes and effect some level of reconciliation while simultaneously defending their conduct between 1861 and 1865 is a rather complex, confusing and, at times, contradictory saga. As cumbersome as it might appear, the history of efforts for postwar reconciliation in the Shenandoah Valley helps us today understand how at least a portion of those involved in the Civil War tried to move on after the conflict as well as why the conflict remains such a powerful and potent force.[8]

The story of postwar reconciliation in the Shenandoah Valley also gives greater meaning to the region's battlefields, for they should not be singularly viewed as places where men sacrificed their lifeblood. They are also places where veterans from opposing armies gathered in attempts to find common ground, heal and take initial steps—however imperfect they might be viewed by us today—to reunite the nation decades after the Civil War's end.[9] The efforts at reconciliation also aptly illustrate the astute observation made in 1945 by Julia Davis in her book *Shenandoah*: "In the Valley…the past and the present are coexistent in time…no man walks into the future without both of them."[10]

Chapter 1

"RECONCILE...TO THE CONQUEROR"

S everal months after the Civil War ended, John Trowbridge—a noted author of the time—toured Virginia's battlefields. As a train carried him into Virginia's Shenandoah Valley, he peered out his passenger car window and viewed the aggregate impact of four years of incessant campaigning, numerous battles and occupations by armies of blue and gray. "We passed through a region of country stamped all over by the devastating hell of war. For miles not a fence or cultivated field was visible," Trowbridge observed.[11] As Trowbridge gazed at the passing landscape, a resident of Winchester who was sitting next to him informed Trowbridge: "It is just like this all the way up the Shenandoah Valley...The wealthiest people with us are now the poorest. With hundreds of acres they can't raise a dollar."[12] A correspondent for the *New York Herald* who visited the valley shortly after the war ended echoed Trowbridge's assessment of the region's appearance: "Between Harpers Ferry and Staunton, a distance of one hundred and thirty miles, they have been devastated almost as thoroughly as the valley of the Elbe from the thirty years' war of Germany."[13]

The scene of desolation in the Shenandoah Valley shocked Confederate veterans as they looked at the communities and farms so terribly devastated by the conflict. For Confederate veteran Robert T. Barton, his native Frederick County in the lower (northern) Shenandoah Valley appeared a barren wasteland in the spring of 1865. Barton explained in his postwar memoir: "The fences and woods were wholly destroyed, the stock and farming implements all gone, no crops in the ground, many of the houses and barns destroyed or decrepit from

Author John T. Trowbridge. *Library of Congress.*

long want of repairs."[14] When Confederate cavalryman John Opie returned, the destruction in the valley shocked him. He described the scene simply: "This Valley, which once blossomed as a flower garden, was one scene of desolation and ruin."[15]

To valley residents—a people who, before the war, produced nearly 20 percent of Virginia's wheat and hay crops and almost 30 percent of the Old Dominion's rye crops—the region's economy and lifestyle seemed ruined.[16] Although the livelihoods of so many valley families appeared destroyed, what had not been broken was their resolve to rebuild and rise as quickly as possible from the ashes. As early as August 1866, area newspapers reported that many of the mills destroyed during the conflict had been either rebuilt or repaired and stood ready to grind wheat.[17] Although the Shenandoah Valley had a long way to go on its path to recovery, it made significant strides within one year after the conflict's end.

A visitor to the Shenandoah Valley the following spring seemed inspired by the unbreakable spirit of the region's inhabitants. "It is wonderful, truly wonderful, how the people of this beautiful Shenandoah Valley have rallied from the prostration of war," noted a New York correspondent in May 1867. The journalist continued in awe: "But, without fences to their fields in numerous cases, these Virginians have raised their annual crops, and without fences still to a great extent, there is a good prospect that they will have the largest wheat crop this year that was ever known here, the whole length of the valley, and indeed throughout the States."[18]

Visitors who focused on the recovery of the region's farms and mills saw progress, but when those same individuals entered the region's towns and cities, they noticed an interesting dichotomy. While the Shenandoah Valley's landscape appeared to be physically on the mend due to the hard work of farmers and laborers, the valley's inhabitants—although determined to rebuild—still publicly bore the emotional scars of the conflict. The same New York newspaper correspondent who stood in awe of the valley's physical transformation in the spring of 1867 appeared despondent at the depression exhibited by the area's citizens. Although he observed physical recovery in Winchester, he noted that "the old time gayety of the place is gone. There is no show of fashion on the main street in the afternoon, and among the women seen abroad a fearful proportion are in somber black."[19]

As this reporter from the *New York Herald* journeyed throughout the valley, he noticed the same dejected attitude in every community he visited. "The number of widows in this and all the other towns up to Staunton is large," the New Yorker observed.[20] When the correspondent engaged in discussions with these Confederate widows, he discovered that although the war had been over for two years, they still held a "strong secesh sentiment."[21]

Nowhere was that pro-Confederate sentiment displayed more glaringly than in the Shenandoah Valley's Confederate cemeteries. The creation of memorial graveyards to honor the Confederate dead concerned a number of northern politicians in the Civil War's immediate wake. Some, such as Pennsylvania congressman Thomas Williams, believed that the establishment of Confederate cemeteries would allow the "strong secesh sentiment" to persist, foster disdain among future generations of southerners toward the national government and provide a seemingly insurmountable obstacle to national reconciliation. So adamant had Congressman Williams become that he proposed legislation on June 4, 1866, to prohibit any activities that honored the Confederate dead.[22] Williams's legislation did not gain momentum because a majority of Congress viewed the individuals in charge of the effort to honor the Confederate dead—women—politically irrelevant and no real threat to the Republic's future political stability.

Two days after Williams offered his legislation, the Confederate Ladies' Memorial Association of Winchester observed the first Confederate Memorial Day in the Shenandoah Valley. Held in the under-construction Stonewall Confederate Cemetery, a place identified by one former Confederate as "the Mecca of our people," the place seemed an inspiration to not only the valley but also the entire South. Largely regarded as one of the first established Confederate cemeteries in the South, if not the first (its origins can be traced to early May 1865), the Stonewall Cemetery clearly illustrated that the defeated Confederacy might have to accept the war's results but would not forget those who fought for the "Lost Cause."[23]

Several Union soldiers who served as part of the Union occupation force that remained in the region after the conflict attended the ceremony out

Stonewall Confederate Cemetery under construction. *Author's collection.*

of curiosity. As the Union soldiers walked into the cemetery, they spied the speaker's stand decorated with an arch. The arch bore the simple words: "To the Confederate Dead." Beneath the arch's center hung a dove, the symbol of peace. Beyond the arch, the cemetery bore no decorations that indicated the commemoration of Confederate Memorial Day. Those who participated in the ceremony, however, did not refuse to display Confederate symbols because they wanted to promote the Union but because they had no other choice. Although federal law did not prohibit the establishment of Confederate cemeteries, it did forbid the display of any of the Confederacy's old symbols.[24] Citizens and former Confederate veterans who participated did display a new emblem of the old Confederacy in the cemetery—a large cross of evergreens, which symbolized the blue cross that bore the white stars of the Army of Northern Virginia's battle flag.[25]

The Union soldiers—some of whom had fought in General Philip H. Sheridan's 1864 Shenandoah Campaign—watched intently as the first speaker, Confederate veteran Uriel Wright, walked to the podium. Those Union veterans listened carefully for any defamatory remarks against the government and, perhaps somewhat to their surprise, heard none. A visitor to that ceremony recorded of the tense moment: "The propitious moment had arrived. Many leaned forward to catch the first words of the speaker. What would he say? What could he say, were questions no doubt asked in the minds of many." Tensions eased when Wright opened: "No potentate or power upon Earth can deprive us of the right to mourn for the dead."[26] With these words the Union soldiers seemed satisfied that this was a mere act of mourning and remembrance, not one intended to rekindle the old Confederacy. The Union soldiers left without uttering a word.[27]

Four months after the first Confederate Memorial Day in the Shenandoah Valley, its inhabitants prepared to formally dedicate the Stonewall Confederate Cemetery. The day of the formal dedication, October 25, 1866, began with the re-interment of four Confederate officers: Captain George Sheetz, Lieutenant Colonel Thomas Marshall, Captain Richard Ashby and Brigadier General Turner Ashby. All of these officers had been buried at other places during the conflict but were now used to further consecrate the ground at the Stonewall Cemetery.

Undoubtedly the most beloved of these Confederate officers had been General Ashby. Ashby was killed while fighting a rear guard action in Harrisonburg, Virginia, on June 6, 1862, and valley residents viewed him as the Civil War's first tragic hero in the region. The people of Winchester

An unidentified group gathers around the grave of Turner Ashby and his brother Richard following a Confederate Memorial Day service in Stonewall Confederate Cemetery. *Author's collection.*

manifested their devotion to Ashby when they chose his death date as the observance of Confederate Memorial Day, a date still honored in that city. As the horse-drawn hearse bore the bodies of these four Confederate officers into the cemetery, the U.S. Army officer commanding the post in Winchester, identified in the records as simply a Captain Brown, ordered the flag in the National Cemetery—separated from the Stonewall Cemetery by only a narrow lane—to be lowered to half-staff. Brown's act proved to be the first step on the path to healing the Civil War's wounds in the Shenandoah Valley between Union and Confederate veterans.[28]

Despite this gesture, many former Confederates had tremendous difficulties in burying animosities so soon after the conflict's end. Although challenging to quantify, evidence indicates that former Confederates in the Shenandoah Valley tried to put on a brave face but still grieved for the defeat, loss of property and, above all, the loss of loved ones. Newspapers in the valley conveyed a sense as early as the summer of 1865 that valley inhabitants "have resolved to be, in [the] future, loyal citizens of the United States."[29] That transformation would not occur immediately, however. Valley resident Kate McVicar wrote that area residents who supported the Confederacy could not "reconcile themselves to the conqueror yet, or forget the scenes they passed through," but they would try to move forward.[30] A northern visitor to the Shenandoah Valley observed: "They cannot forgive the North" for the war "in their hearts, but it is not often they allow their sentiments to overcome them."[31]

In addition to a strong lingering Confederate sentiment in the area, visitors to the valley also noted that former Confederates seemed to place much of the blame for the Shenandoah's hardships on one man: General Philip H. Sheridan. Identified by a Shenandoah Valley newspaper in 1870 as "a Ghoul and barn burning villain," Sheridan became the focus of a hatred that still exists to this day in the Shenandoah Valley.[32]

Valley inhabitants targeted their anger toward Sheridan because it was during his tenure in the region that the campaign with the most widespread destruction of private property in the shortest period of time occurred—"the Burning." While Shenandoah Valley inhabitants first suffered the consequence of war by the torch in the late spring of 1864 when Union general David Hunter marched through the region, Sheridan brought the most widespread devastation to the Shenandoah Valley in the autumn of 1864.[33] In the campaign's aftermath, Sheridan reported that his command, between late September and early October 1864, destroyed around 1,200 barns and in excess of 435,000 bushels of wheat, the valley's staple crop, as well as seized nearly eleven thousand head of cattle.[34]

General Philip H. Sheridan. *Author's collection.*

Former Confederates in the Shenandoah loathed Sheridan not only for the destruction committed during the Burning but also for the time of year that he conducted his operation of desolation—autumn. With the devastation to fall harvests, it meant that the region's inhabitants did not have an opportunity to replant and therefore confronted starvation during the winter of 1864–65.[35] John O. Casler, a Shenandoah Valley resident who served in the Thirty-third Virginia Infantry, concluded after the war that it was the timing of Sheridan's operations that brought such terrific economic devastation to the region and thus cultivated such great animosity toward Sheridan. "Poverty stared the citizens in the face, as this was in the fall season of the year, and too late to raise any provisions. Their horses and cattle were all gone, their farm implements burnt and no prospects of producing anything the next year," Casler noted.[36] Henry Kyd Douglas, who served with both "Stonewall" Jackson and Jubal Early in the Shenandoah Valley, recalled that it would be very difficult to forgive Sheridan and his army for the devastation. "I try to restrain my bitterness at the recollection of the dreadful scenes I witnessed…I saw mothers and maidens tearing their hair and shrieking to Heaven in their fright and despair and little children, voiceless and tearless in their pitiable terror," Douglas wrote after the conflict. "It is an insult to civilization and to God to pretend that the Laws of War justify such warfare."[37]

Even individuals who did not live in the Shenandoah Valley held Sheridan singularly culpable for the hardships endured by the valley's inhabitants. Edward Pollard, a wartime editor for the *Richmond Examiner* and one of the earliest advocates of the Lost Cause, lashed out venomously at Sheridan and his army within a year of the war's end for what they had done to the region's population.[38] In his *Southern History of the War: The Last Year of the War*, published in 1866, Pollard portrayed Sheridan's fiery destruction of the Shenandoah Valley as one of the most horrid occurrences in the history of mankind. Pollard exclaimed: "The horror and crime of this devastation was remarkable even in Yankee warfare. They impoverished a whole population; they reduced women and children to beggary and starvation; they left the black monuments of Yankee atrocity all the way from the Blue Ridge to the North Mountain."[39]

One year after the release of Pollard's volume, the publishing house of Van Evrie, Horton and Co. released R.G. Horton's *A Youth's History of the Great Civil War in the United States: From 1861–1865*. In the book's opening pages, Horton, who strongly sympathized with the Confederate cause, informed his young readers that "this book has been written in the cause of Truth…to vindicate democratic and republican institutions."[40] Horton, who characterized President Abraham Lincoln as a tyrannical dictator, had no difficulty unleashing his diatribes against Sheridan's army. Like Pollard, Horton intimated that Sheridan's destruction singlehandedly brought the economic woes confronted by the Shenandoah Valley's civilians after the conflict. Horton contended: "General Sheridan, with the instincts of savage warfare, determined to utterly devastate this beautiful valley...Thousands were reduced to the verge of starvation...and [are] impoverished."[41]

The assertions made by Pollard and Horton do not capture the real essence of warfare in the Shenandoah Valley. However reprehensible Sheridan's actions in the valley might have been, they were not without historical precedent.[42] While many former Confederates placed all the blame for their financial difficulties after the war on Sheridan and his army, at least one former Confederate who called the Shenandoah Valley home—John Opie—had been able to put the destruction into historical context. Opie recognized that Sheridan had done what so many military commanders had done at various points in history.

While Opie confessed that he was "no admirer of the character of Sheridan and no apologist for him," he informed his readers that there had been ample precedent for everything Sheridan had done. "Many persons supposed then, and do now believe, that this was a new mode of warfare, but vastly mistaken they are," Opie explained. "It has been the custom ever since man first made war upon his fellow-man. The Romans practiced it, and so, also did that humane and magnanimous barbarian Hannibal." In addition to examples from antiquity, Opie also acknowledged that operations similar to Sheridan's had been carried out during the American Revolution. "In our own Revolutionary War," Opie wrote, "both sides devastated the country which they did not wish their enemies to occupy. The British laid waste our Virginia sea coast...and we destroyed forage and provisions in the old central States, to hinder and prevent the British from entering into the interior."[43]

Opie did not stand alone in his quest to place Sheridan's Burning into proper historical context. Fellow Confederate veteran John O. Casler concluded somewhat nonchalantly about Sheridan's destruction: "Such is policy in war."[44]

Although Opie and Casler had been able to put Sheridan's Burning into historical context and showed, as Confederate veterans, a remarkable amount of historical objectivity, they had not been able to fully capture the nature of conflict in the Shenandoah Valley and the war's impact on the region's landscape. Throughout the Civil War, the Shenandoah Valley witnessed incessant military action. The valley's role in supplying foodstuffs to Confederate forces in Virginia, coupled with its transportation centers, its role as an avenue of invasion for Confederate forces into the North and its location as a point from which Union forces could block such a maneuver and at the same time protect Washington, D.C., made the valley a magnet for armies of blue and gray throughout the conflict. A study conducted by the National Park Service noted that the Shenandoah Valley—in addition to numerous occupations by both armies—experienced at least 325 engagements, battles, raids or skirmishes during the Civil War.[45] With the large majority of those engagements having occurred prior to Sheridan's Burning in the autumn of 1864, few parts of the Shenandoah were "beautiful" as R.G. Horton suggested by the time the Army of the Shenandoah tramped into the region.

Seemingly endless accounts exist that portray the Shenandoah Valley as significantly damaged by the time Sheridan began his campaign of destruction. For example, when Lieutenant James J. Hartley, an officer in the 122nd Ohio Infantry, first set eyes on Winchester and its environs in early 1863 as part of General Robert H. Milroy's occupation force, he was shocked at the amount of destruction that had already been done to the region. "A few days ago I took a walk through the ruins of Winchester to see what had been destroyed here. I had no idea that so much had been burned up," Hartley penned his family in Ohio.[46] Around one year after Hartley observed the destruction in the valley, sketch artist James Taylor, attached to Sheridan's Army of the Shenandoah, noted in early August 1864 that so many of the towns and farms already seemed devastated by the conflict. When Taylor came to Middletown, Virginia, and the area around Belle Grove—the scene of the Battle of Cedar Creek—the destruction already endured by its inhabitants seemed appalling. Taylor observed: "The scattering of dwellings and fences at the suburbs [were] literally peppered with Minnie [sic] balls…Belle Grove House was seldom without a military tenant nor its ground without an army. Dead to sentiment, ruthless war had already made a waste of these ornate grounds in which its warrior lord had once taken such pride."[47] On September 3, 1864, several weeks after Taylor's observation, Confederate artillerist Creed Thomas Davis wrote in his diary that when General Jubal Early's army halted near Woodstock, the landscape around the Shenandoah County community had been devastated from incessant use throughout the conflict. "Having been used…ever since the war began, alternately by ours and [our] enemies [sic] army…the country is very destitute," Creed observed.[48]

In addition to anecdotal evidence, a survey of claims for compensation filed with the Southern Claims Commission after the war reveals that while Sheridan's army destroyed much, the valley's population had already suffered from privations perpetrated by Union and Confederate armies before Sheridan arrived in the Shenandoah Valley. Among those who filed a claim after the war was John Geil, a resident of Rockingham County—a region targeted by Sheridan during the Burning. Geil noted in his claim that while Sheridan's cavalry seized more than $600 worth of livestock in the autumn of 1864, Confederate soldiers had placed a heavy burden on his pasture land and destroyed all his wooden fences during earlier parts of the conflict.[49] Fellow Rockingham County resident Henry Showalter noted in his report to the Southern Claims Commission that while Sheridan's army took a horse, saddle and bridle, Confederate forces had commandeered all of his hay, grain and other produce prior to Sheridan's operations.[50] In Kernstown, located just south of Winchester, Samuel Pritchard—whose farm stood at the epicenter of two major battles and numerous skirmishes and served as camps for both sides during the conflict—reported in his claim that he suffered nearly $6,000 worth of damage from both armies during the conflict. In addition to hardships suffered by the Pritchards, when their farm served as part of Sheridan's Camp Russell in November and December 1864, Pritchard noted that soldiers from Stonewall Jackson's command took a great deal from his farm in November 1861—items commandeered without Pritchard's consent.[51]

The examples of Geil's, Showalter's and Pritchard's claims are not intended to exonerate Sheridan for his destruction in the valley and minimize the adverse impact that devastation had on the region's population. They are meant to place the destruction of the valley into historical context. While the devastation caused by the Burning and its impact on valley families should never be diminished, it should be understood that Sheridan's campaign exacerbated an already bad situation for area residents, but it did not singularly create it. Unfortunately for Sheridan's reputation among the valley's inhabitants, his campaign of destruction came last and occurred at the time of year when the valley's population did not have an opportunity to immediately rebuild due to the looming winter. His place as last in line of Union commanders to bring destruction to the valley, the timing of his campaign and the fact that Sheridan's devastation was the most widespread made him the perfect target for those valley civilians who looked for one specific individual to blame for their hardships.

In addition to the hatred that many of the valley's former Confederates felt toward Sheridan after the war, the region's ex-Confederates also despised area inhabitants who retained their loyalty to the Federal government throughout the Civil War—Unionists. In the immediate months that followed the Civil War's end, Shenandoah Valley Unionists attempted to organize meetings that promoted national healing and support for the Federal government.

Each time they did so, former Confederates who refused to accept the war's results and support the government did all they could to prevent those meetings. For example, in March 1866, a meeting of Unionists was held in Frederick County. Several former Confederates showed up to disrupt the meeting and even threatened physical violence should the meeting happen. Still, the Unionist supporters urged those who wanted to heal the wounds of war to not be afraid as they were "now, of the dominant party" and will not "succumb because threatened with violence or injury of property. This war has not been fought for naught, that Union men cannot now discuss political affairs openly and without danger. They will no longer be intimidated by threats either open or covert, nor by sneers, nor by scorn, nor by insult."[52]

Around one month later, the *Winchester Journal* attempted to be the voice of reason in the area and discourage any further violence. "It is time such foolishness as this was stopped," the *Journal* urged. "If men will not learn after the experiences of the last four years, some direct efforts should be made to show them that threats...and bombastic rant are criminal in the extreme...who can tell that it will stop short of future bloodshed...These men...keep open the old wounds."[53]

The *Journal's* words apparently carried little weight in the war's immediate aftermath. Nearly one year after the newspaper urged restraint of attacks against Unionists, the president of Brown University, Dr. Barnas Sears, visited the lower Shenandoah Valley. Sears noted that parts of the Shenandoah still bore not only the war's physical scars but the emotional ones as well. He encountered a number of former Confederates who he stated were filled with such Confederate pride that they intended to do everything in their power to stand in the way of rebuilding and national healing. "Who are these great ones who scorn contact with the Yankees? They are the poor and proud, who whine about the injustice of being beaten in a contest which they themselves provoked," Sears wrote. "And [they] complete their misery by turning their backs upon the only men...who can restore their prosperity."[54]

Hatred for Unionist sympathizers in the conflict's aftermath reached its crescendo in the same year that Dr. Sears visited the lower valley when area inhabitants learned that one of those Unionist sympathizers—Rebecca Wright—had served as a spy for General Sheridan.

When Sheridan took command of the Army of the Shenandoah in early August 1864, he had been cautioned by both President Abraham Lincoln and General Ulysses S. Grant to not bring on a premature engagement with General Early and "risk disaster."[55] Both Lincoln and Grant understood that another Union disaster in the Shenandoah Valley would not bode well for Lincoln's chances of reelection in November. However, after more than one month of military maneuvering between Harpers Ferry and Fisher's Hill, President Lincoln demanded action and wanted Sheridan to "strike."[56] With this pressure and an impending meeting with Grant in Charles Town, Sheridan needed concrete intelligence about Early's exact strengths and any potential his forces had to be easily reinforced.

In order to obtain the necessary information, Sheridan needed someone behind Confederate lines to provide intelligence about Early's positions. General Crook, who commanded one of the corps in the Army of the Shenandoah, informed Sheridan about a potential candidate to assist in their intelligence gathering: a young Quaker schoolteacher from Winchester, Rebecca Wright. To contact Wright, Sheridan utilized Tom Laws, an African American man from Millwood in Clarke County who had a pass from Confederate authorities in Winchester to enter Winchester three times a week to sell produce to residents and Confederate soldiers.[57] In the early hours of September 16, Laws carried a note from Sheridan to Wright. The note stated simply: "I learn from Major-General Crook that you are a loyal lady, and still love the old flag. Can you inform me of the position of Early's forces, the number of divisions in his army, and the strength of any or all of them, and his probable or reported intentions? Have any more troops arrive from Richmond, or are any more coming, or reported to be coming?"[58]

When Wright greeted Laws that morning at her home in Winchester, she was stunned and initially did not know what to do. Although her loyalties rested with the Union, she fully understood the potential consequences should anyone find out about her role in intelligence gathering for Sheridan's command. "Enemies were on all sides of her," recalled a newspaper reporter, "her own sister was believed to sympathize

Rebecca Wright. *Author's collection.*

more strongly with the south than with the Union."[59] After much consideration, Wright decided to provide Sheridan with what little information she had—that a division under General Joseph Kershaw and an artillery battalion commanded by Major Wilfred Cutshaw had departed the Shenandoah Valley to support the Army of Northern Virginia's operations in front of Petersburg.

The information Wright provided, coupled with additional reports from Sheridan's scouts about the disposition of Early's forces throughout the lower Shenandoah Valley, bolstered Sheridan's confidence and became the impetus for his attack at Winchester on September 19, 1864.[60] After Sheridan's success at the Third Battle of Winchester, the first stop that Sheridan made in Winchester was Wright's home on North Loudoun Street. Following his meeting with Wright, Sheridan asked her what he could do for her in appreciation for her efforts in supplying information that greatly shaped his strategic vision and led to the Army of the Shenandoah's military success. Wright asked Sheridan to not tell anyone of her involvement at least until after the war. She knew that if this information leaked out during the war that her life "would be worthless if it should become known in Winchester that I had furnished the information which had resulted in the defeat of Early."[61] Sheridan kept his promise and her anonymity remained secure until 1867.

In January 1867, Sheridan decided to convey his gratitude to Wright by sending General James Forsyth to Winchester to deliver a gift and note in appreciation for her services. Penned on January 7, 1867, Sheridan wrote to Wright from New Orleans: "You are probably not aware of the great service you rendered the Union cause by the information you sent me...a few days before the battle of the Opequon. It was upon this information that the battle was fought and probably won...I will always remember this courageous and patriotic action of yours."[62] An "elegant gold watch... brooch...of gold, beautifully wrought into a gauntlet, and set with pearls" accompanied the note.[63] Although the note and watch exhibited Sheridan's appreciation for her services, it also marked Wright as a spy for the person detested most by former Confederates in the Shenandoah.

Although undoubtedly moved by the gesture Wright knew that this gift needed to remain a secret. This, however, proved difficult. Despite pleas from her mother, Rachel, to keep Sheridan's gift a secret and never discuss it or show it to anyone, Wright could not control her desire to wear the gift—even in public.[64] "I wear these keepsakes constantly," Wright wrote after she received the present.[65] In addition to her reckless display of the watch, a second factor made it nearly impossible to maintain secrecy: a newspaper reporter from the *Baltimore Sun* who boarded at the Wright home on North Loudoun Street. Curious as to who provided the gift, the correspondent began to pry into the reason for Forsyth's visit and the gift-giver's identity. Incautiously, Rebecca's sister Hannah—a Confederate sympathizer during the conflict—revealed the gift came from Sheridan.[66]

By February 20, 1867, residents of Winchester and the Shenandoah Valley learned about the gift and Wright's role in espionage for the detested Sheridan. The *Winchester Times* revealed that Wright "received as a present from General 'Barn burning,' Sheridan, an elegant gold watch, and exquisitely wrought chain, a brooch and charms...The present it is said, was made in recognition of an act, which for the sake of Virginia women shall be nameless in these columns."[67]

The reaction to Wright's receipt of this gift made manifest the hatred that Shenandoah Valley inhabitants held for Sheridan after the conflict. The Washington correspondent for the *Cincinnati Commercial* believed as much when he wrote: "Winchester and Sheridan are names forever linked together. The people who hated the stars and stripes then do not love Little Phil now."[68] A correspondent for the *New York Times* working in the Shenandoah Valley noted that when people in the valley discovered Wright's connection with Sheridan "the quiet of this little place" changed "to liveliness."[69] Wright recalled of the reaction of the area's citizens: "Most of the community were wild with indignation."[70] While the reaction of former Confederate sympathizers was understandable, the reaction of some former Unionist sympathizers, too, was one of dismay. Unionists could not believe that this quiet Quaker schoolteacher had the courage to do something as daring as serve as a spy. "The Union people gathered around me in astonishment," Wright explained. "I remember an old man in the place who took both my hands in his and said, Why, my little, girl, there was not a man in the place who would have dared do such a thing. As much as I like the Union, I would not have had the courage."[71]

Once people learned of her role as Sheridan's spy, Wright—along with the other members of her family—was "socially castrated by the people of Winchester." People boycotted the Wright's boarding home, and anytime Wright dared show her face in public, people shouted harsh expletives and displayed their disdain toward her. Wright recalled that even "the boys used to spit at me on the street."[72] The story of the gift made headlines around the country. While she received sympathy from the northern press, the valley's citizens extended her no such courtesy. They deemed Wright a traitor and wanted her to leave the valley immediately.

Wright and her family left Winchester and headed to Philadelphia. After struggling financially there, Wright appealed to Sheridan for assistance. With the aid of General Ulysses S. Grant, Sheridan secured Wright a position as a clerk in the U.S. Department of the Treasury on July 6, 1868, for the woman he believed "was one of the genuine heroes of the war."[73] She held her post in the Treasury Department until her death in 1914.[74]

Hatred toward Sheridan and anger over Rebecca Wright's involvement made it appear that the Shenandoah Valley's former Confederates might never emotionally recover from the Civil War. Five years after the war ended, however, something occurred that undoubtedly reminded former Confederates not only in the valley but also across the country that former enemies should make some effort to reconcile—the death of General Robert E. Lee.

After Lee perished on October 12, 1870, individuals across the United States largely perceived Lee—as historian John R. Neff has pointed out in his seminal book *Honoring the Civil War Dead*—as a shining example of how a former Confederate could accept the war's results, move on with life and forgive former rivals.[75] The eminent Civil War scholar Charles Roland noted that "Lee lost the war with grace...urged his fellow southerners to accept the verdict of the battlefield...and heal...the wounds of war."[76] While some scholars, such as Elizabeth Varon, have convincingly shown that this interpretation of Lee as always forgiving and gracious in defeat is not entirely genuine—Lee did not always embrace elements of healing, forgiveness and reconciliation—the reality is that whether genuine or fabricated, in the context of 1870, many people believed Lee embodied all of those qualities. In the aftermath of Lee's death, writers and orators did all they could to portray Lee as a proponent of forgiveness and national reconciliation.[77] Lee, who once informed a friend in the summer of 1866 that he "recommended" reconciliation "to others," was heralded by one Shenandoah Valley newspaper after his death as "one of Nature's noblemen...one of the greatest and best that ever adorned the historic pages of any people or country."[78]

When former Confederate turned U.S. congressman John W. Daniel delivered the keynote address at the dedication of Edward Valentine's impressive recumbent statue at Lee Chapel on the campus of Washington and Lee University in Lexington, Virginia, thirteen years after Lee's death, he informed those in attendance that Lee did not forget or encourage people to forget their Confederate past but urged people to not live in the past. Daniel noted: "Lee thoroughly understood and thoroughly accepted the situation. He realized fully that the war had settled, settled forever, the peculiar issues which had embroiled it." To Daniel, Lee served as the model of reconciliation that others should emulate. "Lee had nothing in common with the little minds that know not how to forgive," Daniel stated. "His was the land that had been invaded; his, the people who were cut down, ravaged and ruined...Yet Lee forgave, and counseled all to forgive and forget."[79]

Additionally, 1870 proved a significant year on the path to recovery, as statistically it marked a recovery in the valley's population. By the time of the 1870 census, the Shenandoah Valley's overall population actually exceeded prewar levels. Only a few counties in the Shenandoah Valley—Warren, Rockbridge and Clarke—showed an overall decrease in population from 1860 to 1870. Although one might surmise that this decrease in population illustrated the war's

Robert E. Lee. *Library of Congress.*

devastating impact on the valley's population, a closer examination of census data illustrates that much of the population decline was due to the departure of African Americans from the Shenandoah Valley by 1870.[80]

African Americans, particularly those who were slaves prior to the Civil War, understood that although constitutionally free, they could not enjoy true freedom in an area where people regarded them as unequal. One year after the Civil War's end, George W. Taylor, the postmaster of Winchester, believed that former Confederates in the Shenandoah Valley harbored tremendous animosity toward those freed by Union victory. Taylor wrote that former Confederates' "feelings...towards the freedmen, are more hostile to-day than they were at the close of the rebellion."[81] A resident of Warren County noted that after the Civil War, although the Shenandoah Valley's slaves had been emancipated and African Americans granted equality under the law, "the negro is in all those personal characteristics…as much a slave to-day as he was before the Civil War."[82]

In addition to population recovery by 1870, that year proved an important step on the path to healing the Civil War's wounds for former Confederates because of a political shift in the Old Dominion. Statewide elections in 1870 replaced pro-Union politicians with more conservative-minded individuals. With the threat of sweeping Republican rule now diminished, former Confederates in the Shenandoah Valley believed that there would be few challenges to honoring their Confederate history. This level of comfort took them from a defensive posture to one that would allow them to begin their journey on the path to forgive, if not forget.[83]

The early 1870s also offered another sign that illustrated former Confederates' willingness to not only live with the war's results but also allow Union veterans in the valley to gather and honor their role in the Civil War—the formation of a Grand Army of the Republic post (GAR) in Winchester. Created in 1866, the Grand Army of the Republic became the largest postwar Union veterans' organization.[84] In addition to its work of honoring Union veterans, the GAR also wielded enormous political weight in the country. After the conflict's end, posts sprang up all over the North, but in the South, GAR posts were not as prevalent largely because in the Civil War's aftermath, many former Confederates viewed the GAR not as a veterans' organization but rather as a radical political element meant to inflict Republican rule over the South.[85] Despite these seemingly insurmountable obstacles in sentiment, one Grand Army of the Republic post formed in Virginia's Shenandoah Valley—the Colonel James Mulligan post. One of thirty-five GAR posts in Virginia, it was organized on July 27, 1871. Named in honor of Colonel Mulligan, who perished from wounds received at the Second Battle of Kernstown in July 1864, the post met the fourth Saturday of each month in Winchester.[86] Material on the post in either meeting minutes or newspapers is virtually nonexistent; however, evidence in newspapers indicates that the post met regularly and attended official functions well into the early twentieth century.[87]

Four years after the establishment of the Mulligan GAR post, valley residents and, in turn, the country took another step toward reconciliation as the United States commemorated the centennial of its birth. Ceremonies held in Massachusetts in 1875 marking the opening salvos of the American Revolution included not only Union veterans but Confederate ones as well. Former Confederate general Fitzhugh Lee, the nephew of the supreme Confederate commander, attended the ceremonies in New England despite the censure he received from former Confederate general and, at the time, president of the Southern Historical Society, Jubal A. Early. In the estimation of historian William Blair, Lee the Democrat attended the events as he believed that national reconciliation could also become a useful tool in defeating Republicans. To refuse reconciliation and participation in the nation's centennial meant that Republicans would have all kinds of political ammunition to sling at their Democratic opponents in ensuing elections.[88]

As the country approached 1876 and the 100th anniversary of the Declaration of Independence, former Confederates not only celebrated the signing of the Declaration—the first time they had done so since the outbreak of hostilities—but also actively participated in commemoration events in Philadelphia. Among the former Confederates to make the trip were veterans of the West Augusta Guard—a unit from the Shenandoah Valley.[89]

The year 1876 marked not only the centennial of independence from the British Empire but also a presidential campaign year. In the election of 1876, one of the most controversial in the nation's history, the Republican candidate Rutherford B. Hayes emerged victorious. Hayes, viewed by many as the candidate of national reconciliation, promised officials in the South that if given the election, he would make a number of reforms—chief among them withdrawing any remaining federal troops from the South, thus effectively ending the period of military Reconstruction. Following Hayes's rather controversial yet successful bid for the presidency, he determined to do all he could to heal the war's wounds.[90]

Among the vehicles Hayes used to convey his sense of reconciliation's importance were visits to various parts of the South. In the autumn of 1878, President Hayes, a Union veteran who commanded a division for much of Sheridan's 1864 Shenandoah Campaign, visited the Shenandoah Valley.

On October 16, 1878, Hayes visited and spoke at the Frederick County Agricultural Fair. Now one of the former conquerors of the Shenandoah Valley stood on a stage, ready to be introduced by Frederick William Mackey Holliday, a former colonel of the Thirty-third Virginia Infantry and current governor of Virginia. When Hayes opened his speech, he reminisced about his wartime experiences in the valley. "My first knowledge of the beautiful and historic Valley of the Shenandoah was obtained in the rough school of the Great Civil War," Hayes commented.[91] In a true tone of reconciliation, Hayes did not want to say anything that might alienate his listeners, and so he paid tribute to commanders of both sides for the intelligence they exhibited during the campaigns in the valley. Hayes portrayed the war in the valley as a classroom and regarded the generals of blue and gray as "very

Rutherford B. Hayes. *Library of Congress.*

competent instructors engaged on opposite sides of that terrible conflict." Additionally, Hayes portrayed his visit to the valley and to the battlefields not as an exercise in conquest but as one of reflection. "It is a great satisfaction to revisit the Valley, and to refresh my recollection of its superb scenery," Hayes remarked, "and of the places made interesting and famous by the war. I now meet its people under circumstances far more auspicious than any of us, whether we were soldiers or citizens during the contest, could then have deemed possible within the period of our lives."[92] Still aware that animosity existed in general across the South in former Confederates, Hayes looked to the Shenandoah Valley as an example of how the wounds of the Civil War might be healed—at least among white Union and Confederate veterans—and some level of reconciliation achieved. "Whatever evidences of the old bitterness may be exhibited in any other part of the country, we know that here the general wish is that the sectional controversies which have so long disturbed our American society may be permanently settled; and that in pursuance of the Constitution and the laws, peace and union may be restored and forever firmly established."[93]

Although Hayes believed the Shenandoah Valley could serve as a shining example of how national reconciliation could be realized, the valley's inhabitants carefully showed that as they moved forward, they did not want people to misinterpret increased loyalty to the United States as a willingness to forget their past and let the memories of those who perished in battle fade. During the Confederate Memorial Day commemoration in the Confederate cemetery in Staunton in 1878, the speaker, H.L. Hoover, noted that just because former Confederates exhibited increased loyalty to the Union, they did not have to dismiss their Confederate past. Hoover stated: "There is nothing in the warmest devotion to home, country, or State, or section, at all inconsistent with the utmost loyalty to this Union."[94]

The following year during the dedication of the monument to the Confederate unknown in Winchester's Stonewall Cemetery, the keynote speaker—the Honorable John T. Morgan—pushed the spirit of reconciliation further. As Morgan stood in the shadow of the impressive monument to the unknown dead manufactured by Thomas Delahunty's Laurel Hill Marble Works of Philadelphia, he used his address to further cement the bonds of union.[95] Around Morgan on the speaker's platform were a number of high-profile former Confederates, including General Joseph E. Johnston. In rhetoric typical of reconciliation, Morgan noted that the monument had been erected to honor the "American citizen fighting for conscience sake as an American soldier."[96] Morgan did not believe that future generations had the right to judge soldiers who "fought with true courage and have thus exhibited their honest devotion to the cause for which they have contended."[97] With great reverence for not only the Confederate dead but also the Union dead who rested in the neighboring Winchester National Cemetery, Morgan honored the courage of both sides: "Face to face they fell in mortal combat, and now they rest in peace near each other. Would that those who have survived them were now as reconciled as they are; that our feelings of fraternal regard and our sympathies could mingle as freely and as peacefully as do the ashes of these honored dead."[98]

In closing his lengthy remarks, which included a discussion of slavery's role in the ignition of civil war and why former Confederates should not be regarded as traitors, Morgan offered words of encouragement to continue to heal the war's wounds. While Morgan recognized that veterans might differ over the war's causes and skew the war's history in their favor for the purposes of

Monument to the unknown Confederate dead, Stonewall Confederate Cemetery, Winchester. *Photograph by author.*

personal legacy, they should not let those differences in perspective be an impediment to national unity. "But whether or not we shall agree in the reading of these lessons," Morgan stated, "we shall never forget that they are drawn from the graves of men who were brothers in blood, and who died under different banners believing that they died for right. But one flag floats now, in authority over this city of the dead, and that flag now commands our allegiance as fully, and would as faithfully receive our support in battles, as those banners now furled forever." With the presence of some U.S. flags at the ceremony, Morgan looked out among the crowd and sternly asserted: "Ours is no longer a divided country. No cause of sectional strife remains to divide us hereafter. And we believe…that our form of government is the best, and is founded upon the living principles of truth and justice that this will be a lasting Union of States, under one Federal Constitution and one flag."[99]

Proving that Morgan's words had meaning and were not just empty rhetoric, the Confederate Memorial Day observance in that same cemetery one year later offered tangible proof that at least some Confederates, although they did not forget it, were not stuck in the past. On Saturday, June 5, 1880, nearly fifteen thousand people gathered in the Stonewall Cemetery to honor the Confederate dead and dedicate a monument to the Maryland Confederate soldiers who rested there. Stonewall Jackson's widow, Mary Anna, attended the ceremony and was introduced by Governor Holliday to the survivors of the Stonewall Brigade. After that moving episode, former Confederate general Bradley Johnson spoke and then presented the flag of the First Maryland (U.S.) to General John Kenly.

During the Battle of Front Royal on May 23, 1862, Kenly's First Maryland (U.S.) garrisoned Front Royal. When Stonewall Jackson discovered that Marylanders occupied the town, he summoned Colonel Bradley Johnson's First Maryland (CSA) to the front to lead the attack. Kenly's forces were routed and the regimental standard captured. Now, eighteen years after Kenly was wounded at Front Royal and defeated, the two former enemies from Maryland confronted each other in arguably the most significant act of postwar reconciliation to date in the Shenandoah Valley, returning a flag captured by Confederates at Front Royal to Kenly. The moment was regarded as a "touching scene" when Kenly "despite the terrible wound he received that day [at Front Royal], still survives for his gallant First Maryland (Federal) regiment."[100] Interestingly, for reasons still not clear, Kenly at the last moment in front of a large audience refused to accept the flag from Johnson. Undoubtedly

Maryland monument, Stonewall Confederate Cemetery, Winchester. *Photograph by author.*

somewhat bewildered by this, Johnson graciously agreed to keep the regimental standard, and at some point around 1900, Johnson presented it to the Museum of the Confederacy.[101]

With outward displays of reconciliation, the cause of national healing, at least in the Shenandoah Valley, took another step in the right direction in 1881 when area Confederate veterans from the vicinity around Luray organized a Blue-Gray reunion slated for July 21—the twentieth anniversary of the First

John Kenly. *Author's collection.*

Battle of Bull Run (First Manassas). In a time when Blue-Gray reunions became more widespread, the ex-Confederates from Luray invited the members of the Captain Colwell GAR post in Carlisle, Pennsylvania, to the valley. When members of the Colwell post arrived in Luray, they were treated "accordingly." Apparently the visit was a success, as the Colwell Post invited the Luray contingent to a reunion the following September in Carlisle. They agreed and attended that Blue-Gray reunion, which included three GAR posts from Harrisburg.[102] Although these early Blue-Gray reunions showed significant advances in reconciliation, the location of these events in home communities and not on battlefields illustrated that although veterans had no problem meeting and reminiscing with former foes, they could not yet bring themselves to unite with one another on the battlefields that defined their legacies.[103]

The early 1880s also marked another crucial step on the path to healing in the Shenandoah Valley—greater economic stability. By 1880, as eminent valley historian Kenneth Koons has convincingly argued, the crop outputs of the region's farmers exceeded prewar levels.[104] In addition to the recovery of the Shenandoah's farms, new business endeavors, such as the establishment of hotels, resorts and healing springs, brought further economic strength to the region. Those various ventures attracted vacationers to the valley, some of whom were Union veterans who fought in the Shenandoah in 1864. A visitor to the Shenandoah Valley in the 1880s noted the Shenandoah Valley's transformation from the site of old battlegrounds into a place of relaxation, recreation and economic vibrancy: "They have a valley rich and fertile and are gradually recovering what they lost." The visitor continued: "Instead of a battle field the Valley of Virginia has been changed to an immense summer resort. Numerous springs and summer hotels dot the mountain sides and there is no more imposing mountain scenery anywhere."[105]

The Shenandoah Valley's evolution from old killing fields to resorts marked an important place on the path toward reconciliation not simply because it marked economic recovery but because it afforded Union veterans an opportunity to see at least a part of the South in a different perspective. Any hope of reconciliation depended not only on the ability of former Confederates to accept the Civil War's results and embrace former foes but also on that of Union veterans to eliminate any animosity they might still harbor toward the South. The fact that the South had, by the early 1880s, become viewed by many Union veterans—as historian Nina Silber once pointed out—as a vacation destination, not just old battlegrounds, helped jettison animosities many Union veterans held toward the South.[106]

With a greater spirit of reconciliation and forgiveness, changing attitudes toward the South by northerners, an improved economy in the Shenandoah Valley and the increased popularity of Blue-Gray reunions throughout the country, the veterans of the Army of the Shenandoah—those who fought with Sheridan in the autumn of 1864—began to see an opportunity for postwar commemoration on the battlefields that defined their legacy in the Shenandoah Valley. Like most Union veterans, they longed to immortalize their fallen comrades not only in town squares and northern cemeteries but also on the battlefields and cemeteries of the South. Against this backdrop, in 1883—nineteen years after Sheridan's successes in the valley—the veterans of the Army of the Shenandoah prepared to visit their old battlefields and honor their fallen comrades. This would be the ultimate test of postwar reconciliation as the Union veterans, once so vilified by the Shenandoah Valley's Confederate population, planned to journey to the Shenandoah Valley for a campaign of remembrance, reunion and reconciliation.

Chapter 2

"Sons of a Common Country"

In the autumn of 1882, a member of the Fourteenth New Hampshire Veterans' Association who fought with Sheridan's Army of the Shenandoah approached the association's officers and suggested that since a spirit of national reconciliation had seemed to emerge by the early part of the decade, the New Hampshire veterans should plan for their 1884 reunion—the twentieth anniversary of Sheridan's 1864 Shenandoah Campaign—to take place in the Shenandoah Valley. Soon, the New Hampshire veterans put together a plan and itinerary and published it in one of the most prominent New England newspapers, the *Boston Herald*, in an effort to alert as many of the regiment's survivors as possible. Although the Fourteenth's veterans saw this as a significant opportunity to commemorate their service not in town squares or local cemeteries but on the battlefields that defined their legacy, the general public seemed to care little about this reunion. One of the New Hampshire veterans recalled simply: "When the first announcement had been made the matter was allowed to drop so far as the public was concerned."[107] While the public showed no interest in the New Hampshire veterans' endeavor, veterans of Sheridan's campaign who did not serve in the Fourteenth New Hampshire viewed this as a tremendous opportunity for them as well. "The idea of such an excursion was entirely novel," recalled a soldier who fought with Sheridan in the Shenandoah, "and at once commanded a widespread approval."[108]

Once the Fourteenth New Hampshire's veterans agreed that the time had come to return to the Shenandoah Valley, Colonel Carroll Wright questioned why they should wait until the twentieth anniversary of Sheridan's 1864 Shenandoah Campaign—why not visit the valley in 1883? Also, due to the increased interest from veterans of the campaign who did not serve in the Fourteenth New Hampshire, the Fourteenth's regimental association "invited all veterans who served in the Valley...who desired to do so to join." Once the regimental association opened this visit to other veterans, some members believed it inappropriate to make this trip under the auspices of the Fourteenth New Hampshire Regimental Association. Instead, many of the Fourteenth's veterans believed a new organization should be established. With this widely expressed sentiment, the Fourteenth New Hampshire Veterans' Association morphed into the Sheridan's Veterans' Association (SVA)—a temporary organization that would oversee a one-time visit to the Shenandoah Valley. Under the leadership of association president Colonel Wright, who enjoyed a lucrative career in labor reform after the war, the association printed and sent out information about the event to existing regimental associations.[109] Throughout much of the literature disseminated to the various regimental associations, the SVA paid close attention to how this trip to the valley would be identified. The reunion was not acknowledged as such but rather was referred to officially as an "excursion." The use of the word *excursion* was undoubtedly aimed at portraying this visit as a vacation-like experience rather than a visit of veterans from a conquering army to memorialize their gallant dead.[110] Clearly, the SVA's leadership understood that rhetoric became the most powerful weapon in the battle for national reconciliation. Information sent out to various regimental associations touted the excursion as "the finest opportunity ever to the veteran soldier, and his friends, to revisit the scenes of his brilliant campaigning under 'Little Phil.'"[111]

Colonel Carroll D. Wright, president of the SVA. *Author's collection.*

In addition to veterans who served in the Shenandoah Valley in 1864, the association opened up the excursion to interested civilians. The SVA's executive committee welcomed "friends of those who wore the blue in the famous Campaign of the Shenandoah; and all who desire to enjoy some of the finest scenery in the country and to traverse several of the most sanguinary battle-fields of the Rebellion are invited to join the excursion."[112] A fee of thirty-six dollars covered the costs for the entire excursion. Ultimately, 192 people registered for this trip to the Shenandoah Valley. Of that number, 148 were veterans, 138 of whom represented twenty-seven New England regiments. The remainder of the excursion party consisted of veterans' wives, sons of veterans and other interested civilians.[113]

The veterans who attended the excursion primarily came from regiments that served in the Nineteenth Corps; however, other units of the Army of the Shenandoah were represented in much smaller numbers. Veterans of the Second Rhode Island and Eleventh Vermont represented the Sixth Corps while members of the Thirty-fourth Massachusetts and Twelfth West Virginia represented the Eighth Corps. Although the Sixth and Eighth Corps were represented, the numbers were paltry. While nothing substantial explains why the veterans of the Sixth and Eighth Corps did not attend the excursion in larger numbers, lack of participation among veterans from those two corps could serve as an indication that while Union veterans were ready to reconcile with former Confederates, they were not yet ready to reconcile with fellow Union soldiers. In the conflict's aftermath, veterans from the various units that composed Sheridan's Army of the Shenandoah attacked one another's reputation in regimental histories and penned scathing articles in publications like the *National Tribune* that attempted to diminish a particular unit's role in battle.

Despite the animosity that might have existed among the various corps that served in the Army of the Shenandoah, most veterans, like the Fourteenth New Hampshire's Francis Henry Buffum, the excursion's historian, viewed this as an unforgettable opportunity. He explained: "It was the opportunity of a lifetime for the veterans who followed Sheridan to victory, to revisit the scenes of their triumphs, to contrast the dreadful past with the happy present."[114] Other veterans of the Army of the Shenandoah agreed. As the date of the excursion neared, the association noted tremendous excitement in anticipation of this historic journey. "The Veteran excursion to the Shenandoah Valley, originating with the Fourteenth N.H. Veteran Association, has become so popular that members of about twenty different organizations which fought under 'Little Phil,' in his triumphant campaign have signified their intention of participating in this first trip of its kind ever

Francis H. Buffum. *Sheridan's Veterans.*

undertaken," recalled a member of the group. "The enterprise finds greater favor among those who served in the Valley than was first expected."[115]

To offer some support and guidance to the excursionists once they arrived in the Shenandoah Valley, William Whitney, who served with the Thirty-eighth Massachusetts and was brevetted to the rank of major for his conduct at the Third Battle of Winchester, prepared a collection of maps—which eventually grew into an oversized book of maps with synopses of all of the major battles in the Shenandoah Valley—to help veterans and guests navigate the Shenandoah Valley's battlefields. "The special difficulty of retaining in the mind the events of the many campaigns of the four years in that region [led me to] prepare these maps…in their present shape hoping they may be of service to others in that regard," Whitney stated.[116] Instead of drawing new maps of the campaigns and battles, Whitney reproduced the maps from two other sources. For maps and descriptions of the fighting in the valley in 1862, Whitney utilized the maps prepared by Jedediah Hotchkiss and printed in William Allan's *History of the Campaign of Gen. T.J. (Stonewall) Jackson in the Shenandoah Valley of Virginia*, published in 1880.[117] For the 1864 campaigns in the valley, Whitney relied on George E. Pond's newly published *The Shenandoah Valley in 1864.*[118]

As Whitney prepared his compilation of maps and association officers plotted out the details of schedules, meals and accommodations, one aspect of the trip might have caused some concern for the Union veterans—how would the veterans be received by ex-Confederates in Winchester, the place that would serve as the base for the SVA's excursion to the Shenandoah Valley? Arguably no town in the valley experienced the Civil War more incessantly than Winchester. Witness to three major battles, numerous skirmishes, raids and occupations—including one by

Sheridan's army—Winchester had gained notoriety during the war as staunchly Confederate.

Throughout the course of the conflict, much of Winchester's Confederate population—namely, its women—clung tenaciously to the Confederate cause and did all it could to exhibit its disdain for Union soldiers. The town's women had been notorious since the early part of the war throughout the nation for their relentlessness in resisting Federal occupation. As early as the spring of 1862, the *Philadelphia Ledger* reported on the rudeness of Winchester's Confederate female population: "Virginia has always boasted of the high tone of its society and the elegance of its manners…with their patriotism, all this refinement and courtesy seem to have fled."[119] When Secretary of State William Seward visited Winchester following the Union victory at the First Battle of Kernstown, he informed President Abraham Lincoln that all of Winchester's "women are the devils."[120]

Union soldiers filled their letters and diaries during the Civil War with plenty of vitriol toward Winchester's Confederate women. For example, an Ohio soldier who was part of the Union occupation force in 1863 noted that the town's Confederate "women are generally worse than the men, they would spit in your face if they dared."[121] These women exhibited no fear. During Sheridan's ride from Winchester to Cedar Creek on the morning of October 19, 1864, the town's women reportedly stood on porches and in upper-story windows making lewd gestures as Sheridan and his staff passed.[122] In addition to the usual disdain they exhibited toward Union soldiers, area Confederate women had another reason to complain about Sheridan's Army of the Shenandoah. In the aftermath of the Third Battle of Winchester, the town's Confederates, despite Sheridan's army bringing in wounded Confederate soldiers to the town, became aggravated when Sheridan refused to let the women go out to the battlefield and see to the proper care of wounded Confederate soldiers who still remained on the battlefield.[123] All of these wartime experiences caused the members of the SVA to ponder how the community that despised them the most would react to a return visit.

When the association's executive committee informed the Winchester City Council of their planned visit, they knew that one negative response could undue all of their planning and kill the anticipation. To their happy surprise, however, Winchester's government embraced the prospect of the excursion. The council immediately organized meetings to discuss not only logistics but also how the city's residents—many of whom suffered because of Union occupation policies—should appropriately welcome the Union veterans. During a council meeting on August 21, 1883, the city leaders adopted a resolution that urged a warm welcome that would foster a positive spirit of reconciliation. The council recognized that the veterans intended to revisit the valley and its battlefields in "peaceful array." The statement urged that the Union veterans be treated not as enemies but rather as Americans. "Mindful of our common origin as a nation, and of the identity of our interests in the free institutions we enjoy, and believing that our hope for the future of our country is an undivided one, we feel that these visitors are sons of a common country, and that their children and ours shall unite with ours in the enjoyment and in the defence [sic] of our national liberties," the resolution stated. In addition to welcoming them as "sons of a common country," city leaders also urged Mayor William L. Clark to "call a mass meeting of the citizens of Winchester, to take such steps as may be deemed advisable in order to extend a citizen's welcome to our visitors."[124]

Mayor Clark, who served in the Stonewall Brigade during the war, created a reception committee of twenty-five individuals, including some former Confederates, one of whom was Lewis T. Moore. A prominent Winchester attorney before and after the Civil War, during the conflict, Moore fought with Stonewall Jackson at First Manassas as a lieutenant colonel in the Fourth Virginia and was wounded. Additionally, Moore let Jackson use his home in Winchester as headquarters during the winter of 1861–62. Moore, who heartily approved of secession and the Confederate cause, stated in 1861 at the conflict's outset that it was every Virginian's "duty to stand by our state" and that it was "wrong not to obey the mandate of our State." He now followed the path of reconciliation as a member of this reception committee.[125] With little time to prepare, the

Mayor William Clark. *Sheridan's Veterans.*

committee issued a call for all residents to support the SVA in whatever manner they could. On September 14, 1883, the day before the veterans departed for their excursion to the Shenandoah Valley, the committee issued a final call in the *Winchester News*: "To Our People—The committee on entertainment of the Northern visitors to our Valley on September 19th, most respectfully asks the citizens of our county and city to donate…grapes…peaches…apples… pears. Also contributions of Virginia hams cooked, chickens either fried or roasted, or alive, if preferred."[126] The committee hoped that area citizens would meet "this appeal with a hearty response."[127]

Although Winchester's elected officials appeared to speak with one voice, some of the city's citizens still harbored animosity toward Sheridan's soldiers. While some did not want the veterans to visit at all, others believed that the time chosen for the visit was most inappropriate—the nineteenth anniversary of the Third Battle of Winchester, the final time the oft-contested city changed hands. A Winchester resident, clandestinely identified in newspaper columns as "Vale," condemned the excursion's timing. The author wrote: "In a slight degree the time of their visit was unfortunate, from the fact that September 19 was the anniversary of the only crushing defeat suffered by the Confederates in the Shenandoah Valley; and to many it seemed as if this visit was meant to add humiliation to defeat." Vale believed that had the veterans chosen a different time of year to visit the region, even more of its inhabitants would have been open to extending them a hearty welcome. "This impression kept many from first offering those courtesies to which they would have otherwise done," Vale contended.[128]

While some of Winchester's citizens privately seethed with anger, the resolutions and public displays of support by Winchester's government to make the SVA's stay comfortable alleviated the excursionists' anxieties about being greeted with ire in the city that once despised them. With relief and appreciation, Colonel Wright penned a brief note to Bentley Kern, president of the city council. Wright thanked Kern for the efforts being undertaken to accommodate the veterans. "I assure you, sir, that the spirit of your resolutions is most thoroughly appreciated by the projectors of the excursion." Wright also informed Kern that he looked forward to the opportunity to interact with Confederate veterans—a group Wright viewed as a shining example of the citizen soldier. "In the same spirit we visit your beautiful Valley, and meet the soldiers of the South as soldiers, not as partisans, to celebrate the valor of American soldiers," Wright asserted. "What more fitting spot for such celebration, than the battle-fields of the Shenandoah, where this valor was most conspicuously displayed by both armies?"[129]

News of the actions taken by the city council invigorated members of the association. A New Hampshire veteran recalled simply: "This courteous and hospitable act of the city which had much reason to still cherish something of the bitterness toward those who had so humiliated her, was deeply appreciated by the veterans, in anticipation."[130] The veterans' spirits were further steeled when they learned that they would not have to rely solely on Whitney's maps to guide them over the old killing fields. A handful of Confederate veterans—some of whom had fought against Sheridan in 1864—agreed to guide their former foes over the various battlefields.[131]

Finally, after much preparation, the men who fought with Sheridan in the Shenandoah started their journey to the Shenandoah Valley on September 15. As the train made its way from New England to Washington, D.C., veterans recalled that this journey had been a much more pleasant experience "than the slow and tedious railroad processions which took the boys in blue over the over their first war route to the capital, when danger and not pleasure was the anticipation of the excursion."[132] The memories of the past rushed rapidly into the veterans' minds as they strolled around Washington and examined places where they had been during the Civil War. For Francis Buffum, it felt as if he had entered into the "domain of unrealities." As he looked around the capital city—"the new and magnificent Washington of the new and magnificent nation"—Buffum noted that "the war was looming up again; the great conflict and its marvelous experiences were to stand forth the sole and grand realities for a week, at least."[133]

After the SVA arrived in Washington, D.C., on the afternoon of the sixteenth, the executive committee met and decided to confer a special honor on the commander of the Nineteenth Corps during Sheridan's campaign—General William Emory.[134] Fully aware of the tribulations and campaigning that Emory had to do to clear his name, which was smeared by the Northern press after the Third Battle of Winchester (numerous journalists blamed Emory for Army of the Shenandoah's delay on September 19, 1864), the committee organized a ceremony and presented Emory with a badge commemorating the reunion.[135] Emory appeared moved by the admiration his former troops exhibited toward him nineteen years after the campaign. One member of the association noted that this had a "marked effect" on Emory and formed a "peculiarly pleasant episode of the trip."[136] After the presentation, Colonel Wright invited Emory to take part in the excursion to the Shenandoah Valley. Emory agreed to make the trip.

After spending the evening of the sixteenth and all of the seventeenth in Washington, the excursionists boarded a train for Harpers Ferry and

General William H. Emory. *Author's collection.*

the Shenandoah Valley. The train cars rolled over ground familiar to all members of the association. The veterans undoubtedly recounted their military setbacks in the region and how General Sheridan achieved victory in a region synonymous with disaster for much of the conflict.[137]

As the trains pulled into Harpers Ferry, images of war rushed back into the veterans' minds. "What an array of humiliations, disasters and contradictions must ever be associated with the name and spot," recalled one member of the association.[138] From the moment the excursion arrived in Harpers Ferry, its members confronted a number of obstacles, including rainy weather and a hike from the lower town of Harpers Ferry to Bolivar Heights—a climb that had been made by many of the veterans during the war. "In the first place the company had to climb that hill which raises as an exasperating bulwark between the lower village of Harper's Ferry and Bolivar," one veteran grumbled, "and what regiment ever marched up that hill with an ever-vanishing summit that wasn't made from Colonel to...corporal?"[139] Some of the excursionists groused about the amount of walking involved once they arrived in Harpers Ferry, and others bellyached about an apparent lack of organization on the part of the association's executive committee. There were those in the group, however, who believed that the personal inconveniences they confronted served as a symbolically fitting way to start their sojourn in the Shenandoah Valley. Some of the veterans thought the experience resembled the bad beginnings of some of the battles in the campaign—notably the Third Battle of Winchester and Cedar Creek. "Was there not a singular appropriateness in this beginning?" pondered a New Hampshire veteran. "This campaign of peace was similar in its first development in the Valley to all of the more sanguinary ones which made it

possible. Each of Sheridan's great battles had an apparently bad beginning," recalled the veteran, "and why should not Sheridan's Veterans begin their magnificent pleasure-tour of the Valley with a dubious episode?"[140]

Soon the men settled into "Camp Birge"—named in honor General Henry Birge, who commanded a division in Emory's Nineteenth Corps during the campaign—atop Bolivar Heights on the same ground where, in September 1862, Union forces under Colonel Nelson Miles surrendered to Stonewall Jackson. Once the men settled into their camp, the GAR posts of Harpers Ferry and Martinsburg converged on Bolivar Heights to provide the first official welcome to the Shenandoah Valley.[141] The following day, September 18, the veterans spent the morning touring the sites around Harpers Ferry. While they visited the sites associated with the campaign and other battles, no one place seemed to attract more attention than John Brown's Fort—the scene of Brown's last stand in his crusade to end slavery. Veterans even chipped away pieces of the brick and mortar to take as souvenirs. One veteran recalled simply: "John Brown's fort had been well chipped at every corner, and the relic freight was accumulating."[142]

After the veterans gathered their mementos of Harpers Ferry, they boarded the train cars and headed for Winchester. The train pulled out of Harpers Ferry around 12:30 p.m. on September 18. As it steamed toward Winchester, many of the veterans' thoughts reverted to the past as they passed by fields where the many battles in the area were fought—fields on which they clashed with General Early's army nineteen years before, fields on which their comrades sacrificed their lives for the Union's preservation.[143] As the northern end of the Third Battle of Winchester battlefield came into view, one veteran recorded: "The train is skirting that terrible, that triumphant field, where so many died."[144]

When the train pulled into the station in Winchester, the sight of that community summoned all sorts of memories for the veterans. "We had been there before, in and out, in the day and in the night, pursuing and chased, running as for dear life," one veteran reflected. "Unionists and Rebels playing shuttlecock through the unhappy town. We had been there before, many of us lying wounded in the warehouses and hospitals; some of us as provost guards; some of us as prisoners; in all shapes, in all plights, Sheridan's Veterans had been in Winchester."[145]

Fortunately for the veterans, Civil War Winchester and postwar Winchester were two different places. Citizens who once cursed the presence of Union soldiers now welcomed their former enemies with open arms as they embraced postwar reconciliation. "No! We have never been in Winchester," recalled Francis Buffum. "You royal good fellows; you hospitable gentlemen; you noble ladies; we never saw you before; we never heard of you! We are wrapt in great mystification...How silly to imagine that we conquered somebody about here some years ago. The tumult, the crowd, the cheers, the splendid welcome! Winchester, we supposed we had remembered you."[146] Indeed, the members of the SVA had been greeted by their former foes with, as a correspondent for the *Spirit of Jefferson* (a Charles Town, West Virginia newspaper) reported, "distinguished honors."[147]

Although pleasantly surprised by the welcome reception at the train station, some veterans believed that if Winchester's citizens had received them with a cold shoulder, they would have understood. The veterans grasped that although the valley seemed to have recovered economically from the Civil War, it might not have yet recovered emotionally from the conflict. A member of the excursion party sympathetically penned: "This courteous and hospitable act of the city which had much reason to still cherish something of the war bitterness toward those who had so humiliated her, was deeply appreciated by the veterans."[148]

A further illustration of the desire for postwar healing was the presence of Confederate veterans from Winchester's Confederate Camp, No. 4. The camp members, along with a host of other town organizations and bands, led the veterans from the train station to the Frederick County Courthouse. "Through crowded streets the procession marched, strange thoughts and conflicting emotions crowding the heads and hearts of the Union veterans as they again trod the rough, familiar pavements of that conflict-battered town," one veteran penned.[149] The column stopped in front of the courthouse—a place that bore witness to the war firsthand as a hospital and prison for men of both armies. It was a remarkable moment as they climbed the steps into this building that once witnessed the rulings of Judge Richard Parker, the man who presided over John Brown's trial in Charles Town in 1859; area citizens advocating secession in 1861; and the shouting down and forcing out of the city in 1867 of former Union general Robert H. Milroy, a man despised as much as Sheridan by the region's citizens. The reception inspired the veterans.

Once the veterans collected inside, Mayor Clark addressed the gathering. With the members of the city council and Confederate veterans sitting in the front of the room, Clark informed the SVA: "You have come, gentlemen, from a distant portion of our country, to visit a battle-field which is in the neighborhood of this city, in which battle many of you took an active and no doubt a gallant part." Imparting notions of reconciliation, Clark told the

A view of the Frederick County Courthouse with the Confederate
monument in front. The monument was dedicated in 1916. *Author's collection.*

crowd that he understood the Union veterans did not come to the valley
"with any feelings of antagonism toward us, nor in any vaunting spirit over
the success of that day. We know that you would not esteem those successes
worthy of your recollection had they not been severely earned." Typical of
postwar reconciliation rhetoric, Clark stated that he admired the "gallantry"
of the Union veterans in battle and expected them to pay the same tribute to
the Confederate veterans. "I am sure you do not grudgingly concede," Clark
stated, "that you met on that field a foe worthy of your steel."[150]

Despite the initially positive tone of Clark's address, he cautioned the veterans that although they had been greeted cordially, they might experience some animosity at various points in the valley. Clark noted that the "woes" of war "have been keenly felt by us, and the furrows left by the war in this vicinity are long and deep. I am sure, gentlemen, when you see this, that you will make allowance for the weakness and frailty of human nature…I am sure that you…with soldierly character, will indulgently regard the feelings of our people."[151] Clark believed that, with time and respectful visits by Union veterans to old battlefields, the wounds of the war would begin to heal. He also informed the audience inside that this excursion that the veterans of the Army of the Shenandoah now embarked on in the Shenandoah Valley would turn into a campaign of reconciliation, helping to erase ill feelings between former enemies. "I am happy, gentlemen, that time is accomplishing its beneficent work," Clark noted, "and that each year, as it passes, is removing the traces of the war and healing the wounds which were received in it…the amenities of social intercourse are smoothing out of sight the recollection of the past…let us press forward to that consummation of peace and good will which all true men must earnestly desire."[152]

After being greeted with a round of cheers and applause, Colonel Wright stepped to the podium to address the crowd. In an expression of amazement, Wright informed the Winchester residents that "we did not anticipate the grand reception extended us by your government and your citizens." In an attempt to reaffirm that the Union veterans had not come to the Shenandoah Valley as conquerors, Wright stated: "We have come into your beautiful Valley for the second time, now with no scenes of war to make our visit memorable, but with peace in our hearts and with prayers for the welfare of our whole country. Nor do we come in any spirit of glorification for the events which transpired here nineteen years ago." Additionally, Wright made every effort to illustrate that this excursion provided an opportunity for soldiers to honor soldiers—regardless of what uniform they donned during the Civil War. "We do come as soldiers, to meet brave men who withstood us manfully in battle," Wright remarked, "and to pay the tribute which the valor of Confederate troops has ever won from the soldiers of the Federal army. The war testified to the world the valor of American arms, and this is all we wish to carry in our memories. Brave men met brave men, fighting for the principle they believed to be sacred, and out of this fighting has come the American soldier."[153]

Although Wright addressed issues of the gallantry of both sides and noted the association's desire to honor heroism, nowhere in his remarks did he address the causes of the Civil War or the role that slavery played in the conflict. Wright's address was exemplary of reconciliation speeches in the early 1880s. While some Union veterans, such as Albion W. Tourgee, condemned Union veterans who refused to publicly acknowledge slavery's role or the Civil War's emancipationist legacy in events like the one undertaken by Sheridan's veterans in 1883, most Union veterans by the early 1880s longed to memorialize their fallen comrades. Those Union veterans understood, as historian David Blight has so lucidly concluded, that there was no greater barrier to postwar reconciliation larger than the issues surrounding the institution that ended with the Civil War. The veterans of Sheridan's army, at least in the context of their 1883 visit, then fell in with the ranks of many white Union veterans who, after the war, were willing to sacrifice discussions of slavery and emancipation in favor of remembrance and reconciliation.[154]

Following the reception, the excursion party made its way to its camp—"Camp Emory." With a large majority of Nineteenth Corps veterans on the journey and with General Emory the highest-ranking officer on the trip, the camp could be named in honor of no one else. While the name served as a tribute General Emory, it had additional meaning for the veterans of the Nineteenth Corps. The veterans camped on the farm of John W. Jarrett, the very same ground where troops from Emory's corps fought against Confederates from General John B. Gordon's division. Camp Emory also provided a view of the Hackwood House, where Gordon anchored his line during the Third Battle of Winchester and fought against Emory's troops throughout the initial phases of the battle. The Hackwood House—still damaged from the battle—stood as a tangible reminder of the terrible fighting in the bloody "Middle Field" and "Second Woods." "Every outlook from the camp was delightful," recalled Francis Buffum. "Near by stood the romantic ruins of the once elegant Hackwood mansion, and every eminence round about had been crowned with thundering artillery" during the battle.[155]

As the veterans established their camp, it was quickly discernable that these veterans still maintained great reverence for the corps in which they fought. Undoubtedly aware of all the postwar bickering between veterans of the Sixth and Nineteenth Corps in a variety of publications, the handful of Sixth Corps veterans who joined the association's excursion displayed the Greek cross of the Sixth Corps with pride. A Nineteenth Corps veteran remarked: "From one of the tents was displayed a Sixth Corps ensign with the well-known and most honorable emblematic cross blazoned upon it.

An 1883 view, looking west toward Hackwood, of the land used for Camp Emory. *Winchester-Frederick County Historical Society/Stewart Bell Jr. Archives, Handley Regional Library.*

Those 'boys' are proud of their corps, and they showed more enterprise than did either the Eighth or Nineteenth Corps, for no emblem of these two appeared on the field."[156]

The members of the excursion party went to sleep at Camp Emory on the night of September 18 fully unaware of how the ceremonies they would hold on the following day—on the nineteenth anniversary of the Third Battle of Winchester—would help further postwar healing in the Shenandoah Valley.

On the morning of September 19, the veterans awoke to throngs of area civilians who came to Camp Emory to participate in the day's commemoration of the Third Battle of Winchester. Among the initial activities that morning were speeches given by various regimental survivors recounting their actions at the battle. Ransom Huntoon, who had been a sergeant in the Fourteenth New Hampshire during Sheridan's Campaign, remarked that this day had been one he had been anticipating for many years. "To be permitted to revisit these familiar scenes, so memorable to us, has, for more than a decade, been the subject of my dreams by night and of my longings by day," Huntoon informed the onlookers. Beyond his own personal satisfaction, Huntoon contended, looking out into a crowd mixed with former Confederate soldiers and sympathizers, that this reunion would "result in binding our hearts more closely together, and will increase the vividness of our remembrance and tenderness of our regard for those who sleep on this consecrated spot…It will impress our children…with the necessity of cultivating the sacred virtue of patriotism."[157]

Colonel Wright also addressed the gathering that morning and noted that former enemies needed to respect one another and the Civil War's outcome to set a positive tone for future generations. "Let this excursion and such as this, and all interchange of fraternal courtesies between the different sections of our country teach our children that men can fight for what to them is truth and principle, and abide by the results, with religious submission, like men and like patriots," Wright pleaded.[158]

After the remarks in the Middle Field, the veterans then marched to the Winchester National Cemetery. For the Union veterans, the ability to stand in a national cemetery that also happened to be part of the Third Battle of Winchester battlefield and recite words of homage and prayer to fallen comrades must have been awe inspiring. For more than a decade after the war, tributes to Union soldiers who fell in battle during Sheridan's 1864 Shenandoah Campaign were confined to northern cemeteries, but now they could be properly honored as reconciliation took hold. Captain Charles P. Hall of the Fourteenth New Hampshire had certainly not lost sight of the moment's significance. Hall noted: "We have stood, on Memorial Day, in the cemeteries of our home-land and done what we could to keep green the memory of those who gave their lives that the Nation might live…We stand on Southern soil; the bones of these dear ones molder in the soil which their life-blood moistened; we place upon their graves flowers plucked by fair Virginia hands beside those brought from the gardens of our…homes… [we] stand here with flowers in our hands and tears in our eyes because loved forms lie buried 'neath this turf."[159]

Following a litany of speeches and the recitation of the roll of the dead in the cemetery, Colonel Wright went to General Emory, saluted him and said: "Gen. Emory, all present or accounted for." Deeply moved by this, Emory moved forward, as one veteran recalled, "with trembling steps" and informed the veterans: "You need no words of mine to add to the beauty and solemnity of the occasion…The dead you honor are indeed and well accounted for. They died as nobly as men can die, and I am proud to have commanded them and you."[160] The entire experience deeply moved the veterans. One recalled: "Never before was I so near heaven as in that cemetery." Another stated simply: "I was never so moved in all my life."[161]

After the ceremonies in the national cemetery, Colonel Wright and the members of the association performed an act that manifested reconciliation's timbre. Much to the surprise of Winchester's citizenry,

A view of Winchester National Cemetery. *Photograph by author.*

Sheridan's veterans formed a column and marched to the Stonewall Confederate Cemetery across the street. As the Union veterans marched into the cemetery and formed around the monument to the Confederate unknown, the veterans could hear curious townspeople question their intentions. While this was the first time most veterans paid homage to Confederate dead in Winchester, for at least one member of the SVA, it was not. General Elisha Hunt Rhodes, who commanded the Second Rhode Island Infantry during Sheridan's 1864 Shenandoah Campaign, visited Winchester's Mount Hebron Cemetery (of which the Stonewall Cemetery is a part) on October 4, 1864, and paused at the graveside service of Confederate Colonel John Funk and offered his respects. "The scene was a sad one, and the people looked at us as if we were intruding," Rhodes confided to his journal. "But I did not feel it would be right to leave and so remained."[162]

Nineteen years later, some area citizens might have looked on the Union veterans as intruders in the Stonewall Confederate Cemetery until Colonel Wright addressed the curious crowd. Standing in the shadow of the unknown monument, Wright noted: "Here lie buried the unknown Confederate dead—the brave men we met on the field of Opequon—but they were brave men, and it is fitting and right that we should lay our floral tributes on their graves…we…come with loyalty to noble lives, to brave and gallant soldiers, and with the prayer for peace on earth on our lips and in our hearts."[163] After Wright addressed the crowd, the veterans knelt while two Union soldiers placed flowers at the base of the monument.

Charles Carleton Coffin, a prolific author who served as a correspondent for the *Boston Journal* during the war, observed the look of astonishment on some of the faces of Winchester's civilians.[164] As the column of veterans marched into the cemetery, Coffin spied an elderly man leaning against the Virginia state monument. He approached the unidentified man. "Some of your folks burned my house nineteen years ago," the elderly gentleman told Coffin, "and made me, my wife and children homeless." After casting up the destruction perpetrated by the Army of the Shenandoah in the autumn of

Charles Carleton Coffin. *Author's collection.*

1864, the elderly man inquired what the veterans intended to do. Coffin informed him that they intended to offer prayers and place flowers on the graves of the Confederate dead. Coffin noted that the man, upon hearing this, put his "hand...up quick to his eyes, there was a convulsive movement in his throat, a heaving of the heart. He turned away to hide his emotion."

As the veterans performed their acts of tribute, Coffin looked out into the crowd and saw "hard faces...faces furrowed by time; faces that had been set like a flint against all reconciliation; but at this moment they were dazed, wondering, astonished faces. The hated Yankee of old decorating graves of Confederate dead! Was it possible? Were their eyes deceiving them?"[165]

Their eyes had not deceived them. Action had now replaced words as the tool for healing animosity in the region.[166] Coffin noted that "tears rolled down the cheeks of some" and that former Confederates who had been "nursing their pride, who have in their hearts refused to accept the results of the war, went out from that cemetery with new emotions." Even the elderly gentleman who informed Coffin that his family suffered property loss during Sheridan's campaign turned to Coffin and said, "I must say that I could not keep back the tears just now when I saw your folks kneel and lay their flowers on the graves." Another area civilian reportedly caught up with Coffin after the ceremony and informed him that, with this act, the veterans of Sheridan's army "have indeed conquered us."[167]

The act of respect earned wide praise from area newspapers. The *Winchester News* reported simply that "the excursionists visited the Confederate cemetery where they also held impressive memorial services and placed tributes on the Unknown Mound."[168] In similar tone, the *Winchester Times* noted: "The beautiful tribute paid to the eight hundred Confederate dead that lie buried beneath the mound, by those New England men, will live in song and story for ages to come...when on bended knees around that mound these two hundred brave men of New England fell with bowed and uncovered heads, was completed a scene that will never be forgotten by those who were present."[169]

Two days later, the SVA's members moved south to explore the battlefields of Fisher's Hill and Cedar Creek. Throughout the morning, the veterans walked over Early's positions at Fisher's Hill and scattered in all directions to retrace footsteps of individuals units. In the afternoon, the veterans made their way to the Cedar Creek battlefield. When they arrived, they gathered at the Belle Grove mansion—the structure that served as the Army of the Shenandoah's headquarters during the battle—and were greeted hospitably by the owner, James Smellie. After the veterans ate their lunch,

One of the ribbons worn by veterans of the Nineteenth Corps during the SVA's 1883 excursion to the Shenandoah Valley. *Author's collection.*

members of each regiment walked the battlefield in an attempt to retrace their unit's footsteps and visited the battle lines of the Shenandoah Valley's most significant battle.

As the veterans fanned out over the battlefield, they encountered area citizens, some of whom appeared to put aside their personal animosities toward Sheridan's veterans. One member of the party noted that when they encountered area civilians who lived on the Cedar Creek battlefield, they engaged in "interesting reminiscences" with some of them. However, some residents used the opportunity to remind the veterans of the Army of the Shenandoah how Union soldiers perpetrated economic hardship on valley residents and how because some Union soldiers stole food out of their houses, they had to go hungry for days.[170] Encounters such as these reminded Sheridan's veterans that although their work of remembrance and reconciliation had a seemingly widespread positive impact, not all former Confederates were willing to forget and forgive yet.

On September 22, the anniversary of the Battle of Fisher's Hill, the SVA broke camp in Winchester and moved south, up the valley to Harrisonburg, where they would spend the day and then begin their long journey home. After the veterans dismantled Camp Emory, they formed up as if on dress parade for remarks from General Emory. "I want to say to you, my soldiers," Emory stated, "that I am as proud of you to-day as when I led you on this field nineteen years ago; and I wish further to say that you have inaugurated an entirely new thing." Emory believed that reunions like this one, at which veterans of both sides interacted positively with one another, went a long way to healing the war's wounds. "You have furnished to the world a novel episode in the history of war. Nothing like this was ever witnessed on this planet before."[171] After Emory closed his remarks, he walked down the line of veterans and shook hands with each of them. The place, the man and the moment deeply moved the veterans, especially those who served in the Nineteenth Corps during Sheridan's 1864 Shenandoah Campaign. Once General Emory had said a personal goodbye to each man, the veterans tried to give Emory a shout, but it was impossible. A veteran of the Nineteenth Corps recalled of that moment: "As the beloved commander turned to go the attempt at a cheer was a failure. There was a choking in the throat—the emotions of the moment could not be expressed in hurrahs."[172]

After the veterans bade farewell to Emory, they made their way to the Frederick County Courthouse to show their gratitude to Winchester's inhabitants for treating them so kindly during their stay in Winchester. In a spirit of reciprocity, Colonel Wright informed Winchester's citizens that their actions of kindness had "conquered" them. "To you, soldiers of the Confederate Army," Wright informed the crowd, "we surrender our hearts, and may God prosper you and yours. With this surrender, however, we pledge you our warm support in every step you make towards the prosperity of the South."[173] Furthermore, Wright told the crowd that the reception of the SVA by Winchester's citizens would be used to inform all in the North that the residents of the valley at least are ready to move forward with the cause of reconciliation. "We shall say that the people of the South are in earnest, that this Nation's greatness is assured, and that Virginia and New England bear the old relations which made them invincible in the councils of old. We adopt the noble motto of your Confederate Veteran Association, and seek to perpetuate the memories but not the animosities of the war. You have won us in every way."[174] After Wright's remarks and the presentation of a resolution on behalf of the SVA that reiterated the gratitude expressed by Wright, Mayor Clark responded.

Somewhat shocked by Wright's notion that Winchester's cordiality had conquered the Union veterans, Clark noted, "We are somewhat taken aback…in hearing you say that you have come into our city this morning to surrender yourselves as prisoners into our hands; for, to be frank with you, we had rather thought that we ourselves were the prisoners—captured by your generous and soldierly bearing."[175]

Clark's comments had not surprised the veterans, but they were shocked when a committee of Winchester's women presented the veterans with a floral tribute as a token of appreciation for their respect for the Confederate dead and aggressiveness in attempting to heal the Civil War's wounds. Francis Buffum accepted the flowers on behalf of the veterans, and just as he had been amazed at the transformation of Winchester's women a week prior, so, too, had this gesture shocked him. "To be remembered by the noble ladies of Winchester in this delightful manner is something I could not have anticipated."[176]

The veterans departed Winchester on September 22 with a sense of optimism for the country's future; however, as they boarded trains for Harrisonburg, some might have wondered how the residents of Harrisonburg and Rockingham County—an area of the Shenandoah Valley that suffered some of the most significant devastation during the Burning—would treat Sheridan's veterans. Perhaps much to their surprise, the members of the SVA, as well as members of the Harpers Ferry and Martinsburg GAR posts who accompanied the veterans on the trip to Harrisonburg, received a cordial welcome by area residents.[177]

The welcome, which included a rousing "yell" that did not mean "bayonets, but brethren," caused the Union veterans to feel comfortable and welcome. The "peculiarly felicitous" welcome was due in large part to the efforts of Colonel D.H. Lee Martz.[178] Martz, an officer in the Tenth Virginia Infantry who had fought against Sheridan's veterans in the autumn of 1864, was regarded as one of Rockginham's leading citizens. Referred to as a man of "unfailing courtesy," people of "all classes" held Martz in high esteem.[179] In anticipation of the SVA's visit, Colonel Martz wrote a "stirring appeal to his veterans to turn out and welcome the New England veterans."[180] Martz's efforts, along with those of other civilians from Rockingham, did not go unnoticed, as one newspaper correspondent recorded: "The citizens of Harrisonburg provided a sumptuous entertainment for the Veterans."[181]

Colonel D.H. Lee Martz. *Office of the Clerk of the Circuit Court for Rockingham County and the City of Harrisonburg, Virginia.*

Veterans of the Tenth Virginia responded favorably to Martz's call, as did veterans from other Confederate units. After the SVA disembarked from the train, they marched to the courthouse, where they were greeted with a rousing reception. Samuel J. Harnsberger, who chaired the Harrisonburg reception committee, issued the formal welcome to the Union veterans. Wanting to convey that they were no longer regarded with widespread hatred, Harnsberger informed the Union veterans: "We desire you to feel and realize that you are not 'strangers in a strange land,' but that you are, one and all, verily at home and in the house of your friends." While Harnsberger recognized the significance of the date as the nineteenth anniversary of the Battle of Fisher's Hill, he noted that it was in the past and now the country needed to move forward as Americans. "To-day is the day of peace," Harnsberger noted, "for all well-meaning citizens and true Americans, and as such we meet together in person, and we cheerfully extend to you and receive from you the right hand of fellowship; and as to all differences we plead the statute of limitation each upon the other."[182]

As the veterans of the Army of the Shenandoah listened to Harnsberger's remarks, they noted that among the decorations rested an image of Stonewall Jackson. With Confederate veterans in the audience representing at least six different Virginia regiments, including some who served in the Stonewall Brigade, one Union veteran shouted out to Harnsberger to raise the picture high so that all in the crowd could get a good look. Harnsberger raised Jackson's image, iconic, and "cheer upon cheer was given, and the air was filled with the waving of hats of the veterans of both armies."[183]

While the call from the Union veterans to raise the image of Stonewall Jackson promoted unity among former enemies, it should not necessarily be construed as extraordinary. While Jackson stood as one of the Confederacy's iconic images—perhaps second only to General Robert E. Lee—and created all sorts of problems for Union forces in the Shenandoah Valley and war planners in Washington, D.C., Jackson had admirers in both the North and South during and after the conflict. Many who sided with the Union during the conflict admired Jackson not for the cause for which he fought but rather for the superb generalship he displayed on the battlefield. Union soldiers; poets, such as Herman Melville; members of President Lincoln's staff; and even Lincoln himself went on record during the Civil War about their admiration for Jackson.[184]

Once the cheers for Stonewall Jackson had subsided, Colonel Wright responded to Harnsberger's comments. Wright acknowledged how the reception deeply moved the veterans and informed the onlookers of how this excursion to the battlefields of the Shenandoah Valley had become an almost religious experience. "We are beginning to understand and appreciate the motives and grant sentiments which actuated the Crusaders of old. We have made a pilgrimage which must have its influences upon the hearts of the people of two great sections of the country. We have come among you with peace in our hearts," Wright stated during his address. Wright also used the opportunity to send a message to veterans of both armies around the country. He acknowledged that although the nation seemed to be on the path of reconciliation, animosity still existed not only among former Confederates but also among Union veterans as well. Wright believed the treatment of the Union veterans by their former enemies in the Shenandoah Valley and the numerous acts of respect displayed for the Union veterans should be regarded as the ultimate lesson in postwar reconciliation. "I wish the scenes of this week could be re-enacted all over our country," Wright stated. "I wish the men of the great contending armies of the Civil War could hold re-unions everywhere, for by such experiences the fact of the Rebellion would fade away, and the impulse of the whole Nation would be towards the Nation's success... your generous bearing in extending to us such hearty welcome is testimony enough to your sincerity, to your brotherly feeling."[185]

After spending the afternoon in Harrisonburg, the veterans boarded the trains for the journey home. That evening, the train made its way north and stopped briefly in Winchester. While this was not a prolonged stay, Sheridan's veterans were surprised at the large crowd of people gathered at the Winchester train station. "These Winchester people are as tenacious in their hospitalities as they were aforetime in their hostilities...An immense concourse greeted us and all the former enthusiasm was more than renewed," recalled Francis Buffum.[186] The train then made its way to Harpers Ferry, where the veterans witnessed a fireworks display put on by the members of the Harpers Ferry GAR post as they passed.[187]

The excursion departed the Shenandoah Valley, and on Sunday, September 23, the veterans stopped for a respite in New York City. The previous week had proved to be a whirlwind of activity, reflection and emotion. As one veteran reflected on his experiences in 1883 as compared to 1864, he thought that "there was a strange pleasantness in the entire affair... the contrasts of a week full of all sorts of contradictions, placing the veteran at either end of the [nineteen] years for his observations."[188] For many veterans, the rest in New York offered the first opportunity to truly assess the significance of their journey. The association's vice-president, Elisha Hunt Rhodes, reflected that the excursion to the valley had changed the sentiment among former enemies. "I believe in sentiment as a wonderful incentive in human life," Rhodes recalled. "Sentiment is sometimes derided, but it is one of the practical impulses of the world. Sentiment develops the strongest and most beautiful qualities in a man. The excursion grew out of sentiment. By its inspirations we have all been quickened."[189] The former governor of Rhode Island A.H. Littlefield hoped that the visit to the Shenandoah Valley would be the beginning of "bringing about a warmer friendship between those who had met in deadly conflict."[190] Rhode Island's secretary of state, Joshua M. Addeman, who had served as a captain in the Fourteenth Rhode Island Heavy Artillery during the war (the unit did not see service in the Shenandoah Valley), viewed the journey as a success for the veterans who wanted to remember fallen comrades. Additionally, Addeman regarded the trip as a positive one, as it altered views of former enemies. "We have journeyed to the Valley of the Shenandoah with varied motives, but all as travelers, expecting only to receive such courtesies as respectable and law abiding citizens are entitled to," Addeman mused. "These we have indeed enjoyed, but how much more! As we recall the generous welcomes from municipal authorities, from the various organizations and communities, and the pleasant receptions at hospitable firesides, we find words very inadequate to do justice to the subject. But the grateful memories will abide with us."[191]

In the Shenandoah Valley, former Confederates likewise reflected positively on the experience. The *Winchester News* noted that throughout the entire visit, the "very best of feelings prevailed." Additionally, the newspaper reported that it approved of the tone of the addresses delivered by various members of the association. "Col. Wright, in his remarks, disclaimed any intention of coming here to celebrate or glorify over any victories of the battle-field but simply to revisit the scenes and places of former service," the *News* noted. Valley residents seemed to approve of the veterans' conduct and fully understood the significance of their visit. "The best order prevailed during the stay of the veterans, and nothing occurred to mar the pleasure of the visit. The behavior of the excursionists is highly extolled by all, and it is to be hoped that the visit will go far toward exciting friendly feelings between the two sections of the country. The visitors expressed themselves as highly gratified at Virginia hospitality," reported the *Winchester News*.[192]

Even some of the Shenandoah Valley's citizens who believed the timing of the excursion was inappropriate expressed positive sentiments about the veterans' visit. A Winchester resident who harbored animosity toward the Union veterans before they arrived penned after their departure that "the generous and manly spirits to which they met the people of the Shenandoah Valley has done more to heal the wounds of the late war than anything else that has happened since its close. They proved themselves…courteous gentlemen, and the generous sentiments they expressed found a ready response in the hearts of our people. A thousand bitter memories of the ravages of war were obliterated."[193]

In the months after the SVA visited the Shenandoah Valley, members of the excursion shared their experiences with other Union veterans and regaled Grand Army of the Republic meetings with tales of the cordiality of the valley's residents.[194] Among those who aggressively spread the message about how the former Confederates in the valley had changed their attitude toward Union veterans was Reverend Benjamin F. Whittemore. The former chaplain of the Fifty-third and Thirtieth Massachusetts Infantry regiments, an ex-congressman and a book publisher, Whittemore addressed several Grand Army of the Republic posts in Massachusetts about the kind treatment Winchester's citizens exhibited toward the veterans. So moved had these posts become that they penned resolutions in praise of Winchester and sent them to the city council. Although it did not occur on a massive scale, the members of the SVA began to alter the mentality among some Union veterans who looked skeptically on the South's willingness to put aside animosity for the sake of the country.

Sheridan's veterans undoubtedly approached their 1883 reunion in the Shenandoah Valley with great trepidation; however, after the visit they, as well as many of the valley's inhabitants, had their fears allayed. Together both Union veterans and former Confederates truly came to realize the importance of reconciliation and the need for healing between former foes. While the SVA showed a course for others in the nation to follow, their campaign of reconciliation

Reverend Benjamin F. Whittemore. *Walter Blenderman/Pat Clevenger private collection.*

had not ended but rather had just begun as they tried to develop new ways to honor their fallen comrades while at the same time cement the Union they fought to preserve.

Chapter 3

"THERE WAS NOT SO MUCH
TREADING ON EGGS"

As the train cars rolled north to New England in late September 1883 carrying the members of the SVA home from their excursion in the Shenandoah Valley, the mood among the veterans proved bittersweet. While the veterans reflected positively on the trip, most had two regrets. First, they did not feel that they had enough time to explore the battlefields that defined their legacy in the Shenandoah Valley. Excursion historian Francis Buffum recalled of this sentiment: "It was already apparent that the time included with the limits of the excursion was altogether too short for any thorough exploration of the battle-fields."[195] Furthermore, each veteran knew that the SVA was created as a temporary organization for a one-time visit to the Shenandoah Valley. During the journey home, however, some of the members proposed that the association remedy their regrets by making the association into a permanent organization, one that would hold annual reunions and hopefully at some point organize a return visit to the Shenandoah Valley. The veterans unanimously agreed, and beginning in 1884, the association began its practice of holding annual reunions.[196]

On December 10, 1884, the now permanent association gathered at the Quincy House in Boston, Massachusetts, for its annual reunion. Although members met in New England's most significant city, the thoughts of the veterans immediately turned to the Shenandoah Valley and the previous year's excursion. During the association's executive committee meeting and the general reunion, the veterans reflected positively on their experience in the Shenandoah Valley. The veterans not only reveled in the personal enjoyment of the trip but also contended that their excursion established a crucial building block in the foundation of national healing. The *Boston Journal* reported that during the course of the Quincy House reunion, a member of the association addressed the gathering and "expressed his belief that by such means more than by any other is the much-desired fraternization between the North and South to be brought about." With such positive reflection and perceived significance to national reconciliation, the association determined that it would return to the Shenandoah the following year and continue its campaign of reconciliation in the valley.[197]

As the association planned for the 1885 excursion, the association's leadership determined that the visit would include the usual slate of reunion activities: memorial addresses, monument dedications, campfires and battlefield exploration. The association's executive committee concluded that these types of activities would continue "to cultivate the acquaintance of, and bind in hearty fellowship, the brave men who wore gray in 1864, who were our foes, are now our friends, and who, by the cordiality of their welcome in 1883, challenged our highest confidence and esteem."[198]

Some members of the association, however, believed that it would take more to cement relations among former enemies than the usual slate of speeches and ceremonies. A contingent of the veterans determined to add a new dimension to the visit, one they believed would provide a crucial building block of reconciliation as well as afford entertainment to veterans of both sides—rifle competition between the veterans of Sheridan's army and Confederates who fought in the 1864 Shenandoah Campaign. When initially suggested, a member of the association's executive committee recalled, "several of the committee looked askance upon this scheme at first, because they anticipated that a contest between those who fought with such sanguinary bitterness on that very ground—and especially with rifles—would revive that bitterness to a degree which would at least chill the relations of those who were old time foes."[199] While this was an understandable reaction, the Fourteenth New Hampshire's Francis Buffum did not believe, based on the positive experience in 1883, "that there was...the slightest foundation for such a fear."[200]

Once anxieties about the competition ceased, various regimental associations that had affiliated with the SVA issued calls for marksmen. The Fourteenth New Hampshire Regimental Association urged its veterans to participate in the rifle competition. A circular sent to survivors of the regiment urged the "'boys from the Granite State [to]...march at the head of the column" in this new endeavor. The call for riflemen, appealing to regimental pride and the spirit of reconciliation, stated: "The Fourteenth used its rifles most effectively in the battle of the Opequon, twenty-one years ago. Again the crack of the rifle and 'zip' of bullets are to be heard on that once bloody field, but now only in friendly competition...The hearty co-operation of all our comrades will bring new laurels to the 'Old Fourteenth.'"[201]

As rifle teams organized and the association's leadership made preparations for this second campaign of reconciliation, Winchester's city council and its residents again eagerly made arrangements for the visit. During the several weeks prior to the veterans' arrival, the *Winchester Times* chronicled the work and anticipation of both sides. The *Times* reported nearly three weeks prior to the visit of Sheridan's veterans that "the enthusiasm over this trip is something phenomenal...Gen. George L. Beal [who commanded a brigade in the Nineteenth Corps during Sheridan's Shenandoah Campaign] reports much enthusiasm in Maine over the trip...A hearty welcome awaits the party from our entire people and many pleasant hours are looked forward to with our Northern brethren."[202]

The euphoria that preceded this second excursion to the Shenandoah Valley did not last long, however. Shortly after the *Winchester Times* published its story of positivity and eager anticipation, the *Winchester News* published a column dropping a bombshell that threatened the entire visit and the work of reconciliation in the Shenandoah Valley. Less than one week before the SVA's arrival, the *News* printed a letter written by an unidentified group of veterans from the Stonewall Brigade. The note simply stated: "We, as members of the 5th Virginia Infantry, Stonewall Brigade, don't want any re-union with any...Yankee regiment."[203] This reaction shocked and dumbfounded the Union veterans.

What puzzled some of the veterans was that the negativity expressed by the anonymous contingent of Stonewall Brigade veterans in September 1885 did not mesh with the widespread attitude that many former Confederates publicly expressed in previous weeks as they showed reverence for Ulysses S. Grant after his passing on July 23, 1885. Confederate veterans penned resolutions and southern newspapers published columns of adoration for Grant. Former Confederate Judge John Paul of Rockingham County—a region devastated during Sheridan's 1864 Shenandoah Campaign—noted that when "Grant, was placed in his tomb all the world mourned his loss."[204] On August 8, 1885, the day of Grant's funeral procession in New York City, several companies of Confederate veterans, including those who served in the Stonewall Brigade, marched in the funeral procession honoring not only a former president and conquering general but also a man who embraced the spirit of postwar reconciliation.[205]

A number of the SVA's members were "outraged by the unwarrantable, unjust, and utterly groundless imputation that the members of the 5th Virginia regiment, Stonewall Brigade, as a regiment, are opposed to holding a reunion with veteran Union regiments."[206] Other members of the association appeared a bit more understanding of the reaction. "It was the most natural thing in the world for a spirit contrary to that shown by the welcoming committee and citizens to be cherished. It was impossible for many to forget the lost cause. One veteran noted: "With all the fiery intensity of their Southern natures, they had devoted themselves to the Confederacy, and how could they be expected to forget the lost cause sufficiently to welcome as friends those who had been their conquerors?"[207]

Regardless of the fact that some Union veterans excused the opinions of certain Stonewall Brigade veterans, some of Sheridan's veterans could not ignore these incendiary remarks. Various political forces as well as Confederate veterans in the Shenandoah Valley who embraced postwar healing did all they could to allay any concerns and make certain the visit would still occur as scheduled. A New Hampshire veteran recalled that the members of the association had been "assured" by veterans of the Stonewall Brigade "that more than nine-tenths of the members of the 5th Virginia repudiate the intimation that they shall indulge in, and harbor enmity and personal hatred to any regiment or regiments of Union soldiers, but have [nothing] but good-will and friendship for their former opponents upon the battle-field."[208]

As some Union veterans stood on the verge of not making a return trip to the Shenandoah Valley due to the comments from the Stonewall Brigade veterans, the *Boston Daily Globe* offered its opinion on the state of affairs. The *Globe* reminded those Union veterans who contemplated pulling out of the trip to the valley that "the memories of the past of course can never be obliterated from the minds of those who took part in the war."[209] It cautioned the SVA's members to be cognizant that even though they may encounter individuals who refuse reconciliation and any form of postwar healing, their excursions to the Shenandoah Valley set an important tone for the nation. "That such excursions result in great good there can be no doubt. They serve to bind together more firmly the people of a once divided country." The *Globe* reminded the veterans that "to teach the children lessons of love of country that will serve in the future to prevent 'discordant and belligerent States from warring against each other'" was the goal they were working toward.[210]

The *Winchester Times* also got involved to make the veterans feel welcome. Its editors urged area citizens to welcome Sheridan's men with open arms and embrace the spirit of reconciliation. "To one and all, we extend a hearty welcome and trust that their sojourn among us may be conducive to great good to all of us, and may strengthen the chords of affection and unity between the sections," the *Times* stated.[211] The newspaper also "desired that a number of Confederates and their ladies…be present and sing the old songs that were so popular during the war…Again we tender the N[ew] E[ngland] Vets a hearty welcome to our beautiful Southland, and trust they may have bright skies and pleasant weather and an enjoyable time."[212] The rhetoric from the valley and advice from the pages of the *Boston Globe* eased anxieties enough to allow the Union veterans to embark on their second campaign of reconciliation in the Shenandoah.

When the 185 members of the SVA excursion party arrived in Winchester on September 16, hundreds of the city's residents and Confederate veterans greeted them warmly, just as they had done two years earlier.[213] At first glance, there appeared no outward manifestation of animosity to this second visit of Sheridan's veterans. "If there was divided sentiment in the Valley as to the desirability of this visit," noted association historian Francis Buffum, "the cordiality, assiduity and delicacy of the Winchester officials and a great number of eminent citizens gave to our reception the full appearance of a unanimous welcome." While this display might have allayed some veterans, others wanted further confirmation that they were indeed welcome again in this region.

As the veterans disembarked from the train, they immediately began to mingle with former Confederates in the crowd in an attempt to truly gauge the sentiment toward this return visit. Some former Confederates informed the veterans that while they embraced a reunion with Union veterans, there were still many in the region who could not reconcile with their army's commander, General Sheridan. "There are many inhabitants of the valley who [still] have no love for Gen. Sheridan," the veterans were informed, "and probably will never forget the devastation caused by his famous order."[214]

After releasing profanities toward Sheridan, the ex-Confederates then informed the Union veterans that even though many would never forgive Sheridan, former Confederates were willing to move with the "tide of progress" and do whatever necessary to advance national healing. One former Confederate soldier informed the Union veterans that he, as well as some of his comrades, had become extremely unpopular with others in the valley who refused reconciliation and would rather remain "at home nursing their venom."[215]

This unidentified Confederate veteran also noted that many of the individuals who snubbed their nose at reconciliation also did so to the idea of serving in the Confederate military during the Civil War. They refused to fight "for the principles they professed to have," and now that the war ended in Confederate defeat, these individuals continue to "live in the traditions of the past." In the estimation of one Confederate veteran, these Shenandoah Valley inhabitants were "no benefit to the civilization of the present."[216] Another former Confederate within earshot of this conversation believed that these individuals who refused to fight for the Confederacy but who now blocked reconciliation had become "copperheads" to postwar healing. "We have in the valley what you called copperheads in the North [during the conflict]…who…now when there is peace all over the land are fostering a spirit of hatred for the North." This former Confederate soldier suggested these southern "copperheads" could do real damage to national unity if their message took hold among the region's children. These postwar southern copperheads viewed impressionable children as an important cog in their campaign to block any form of reconciliation with Union veterans for at least another generation. They "are fostering a spirit of hatred for the North among such young people as they can influence," noted the unidentified Confederate veteran. "Such men have no influence with the ex-Confederate soldiers, but their influence hurts young men."[217]

Following the initial welcome and conversations with Confederate veterans near the train depot, Sheridan's veterans made their way to Camp Russell. Named in honor of Union general David A. Russell, who was killed at the Third Battle of Winchester while commanding a division in General Horatio Wright's Sixth Corps, the semicircular camp of tents stood on the north side of the Berryville Pike (present-day National Avenue) opposite the National Cemetery. As the veterans passed beneath the archway bearing the words "Camp Russell," one solitary cannon fired, and the Stars and Stripes was raised on a flagpole situated at the camp's center.[218]

One of the hallmarks of the 1885 reunion was public interaction with not only rank and file Confederate veterans but also those who held high rank as officers during the conflict—especially those who held enormous political clout after the war and could encourage the masses to reconcile with their former enemies. Among the former Confederate officers invited to attend the reunion was Fitzhugh Lee.

As one of General Robert E. Lee's nephews, as well as a former Confederate general who fought in the Shenandoah Valley in 1864 against Sheridan's Army of the Shenandoah, Fitzhugh Lee's presence at the 1885

The entrance to Camp Russell as it appeared in 1885. *Author's collection.*

excursion had the potential to be a huge boost to national reconciliation. Although a Democrat who upheld the doctrine of states' rights, Lee "proclaimed himself thoroughly national in his sympathies."[219]

Lee's familial connections, Confederate experience and powerful place in Virginia politics made him arguably the SVA's most significant guest. Unfortunately, the SVA's visit coincided with a gubernatorial election in the Old Dominion and Lee's bid for the governor's mansion in Richmond. While Lee promised his participation, last-minute campaign obligations forced Lee to back out of his visit with Union veterans in the Shenandoah Valley. Although one might be inclined to surmise that Lee backed out not due to the demands on his time but rather because he did not want to alienate potential voters who refused reconciliation with former Union soldiers, evidence indicates otherwise. During the course of the gubernatorial campaign Lee, who ended up winning the election, made no secret of the fact that he favored reconciliation with the North. For example, in the summer of 1885, Lee served on General Winfield Scott Hancock's staff during the funeral procession of former military rival and president of the United States, General Ulysses S. Grant. A trusted supporter of Lee noted that it was at that point that "he had realized…the hearty union of the North and South" was essential to American society.[220] Before the SVA's arrival in Winchester, Lee publicly proclaimed that he did not dwell "over the memories of the sanguinary feud that occurred in this country something like a quarter of a century ago."[221]

Members of the SVA gather for an evening dinner in Winchester during their September 1885 visit to the Shenandoah Valley. *Author's collection.*

When Lee backed out of his invitation to join the Union veterans' excursion to the Shenandoah Valley, he went to great lengths to not only publicly apologize but also express his best wishes to the veterans of both sides as they performed work essential to national healing. His note of regret and encouragement was published in newspapers throughout the region. The *Baltimore Sun* reported that when the veterans learned of Lee's inability to be present for the commemoration of the Third Battle of Winchester "great regret was expressed at the announcement."[222] Lee informed Sheridan's veterans: "I regret that my political engagements will prevent my presence upon such an interesting occasion." While Lee used the opportunity to express his regret, he also utilized the opportunity to express the benefits of events in which veterans of both armies participated together: "Such reunions result in producing a fraternal feeling among the sections and strengthening the union of States. The South is marching steadily forward and hopes to do her share towards making this Republic what our forefathers intended she could be 'the glory of American and the blessing of humanity.'" Lee clearly informed the veterans and those who read his published letter that many former Confederates were "not chanting miseries over a struggle of a quarter century ago, but [are] waving the star-spangled banner and hopes the 'bloody shirt' will be furled forever. If the coming of our Northern brethren assists in accomplishing desirable results bid them welcome."[223]

Fitzhugh Lee. *Library of Congress.*

The association planned no official activities for its first full day in the valley. Some veterans used that opportunity to visit Luray Caverns, and others opted to make the shorter trip to Antietam battlefield. Although the veterans who visited Luray Caverns intended for it to merely be a visit to an emerging tourist attraction, the tour contained a tone of reconciliation. Once in the caverns the veterans were taken to a large chamber and treated to versions of "'Yankee Doodle' and 'Dixie' as played by the guides on the strange stalactite organ."[224] One unidentified Union veteran refused to visit either place and instead used the opportunity to seek a Winchester woman who had taken care of him and nursed him back to health. Although the identities of the veteran and the woman were never revealed, the excursion's historian Francis Buffum recorded that a reunion between the two did occur. Buffum recalled of the reunion:

"Never had he forgotten her, and he had proudly showed the bouquet which she had given him at parting, now faded and dry; he the Northern soldier and she the Virginia maid."[225]

September 18 marked the first official day of activity in the Shenandoah Valley as the veterans boarded train cars that carried them south to Harrisonburg, a region terribly devastated during the war and now, twenty-one years later, the scene of a unique manifestation of reconciliation—competitive rifle matches between former enemies. As the veterans rode the rails seventy miles to Harrisonburg, they passed through numerous battlefields that stirred emotions. "Many places were familiar to their vision and [they] commented on it in various ways," noted one member of the excursion party.[226]

The veterans arrived in Harrisonburg slightly before noon. Even though Sheridan's veterans had visited Harrisonburg two years before, their arrival in 1885 still stirred tremendous emotions in people who either experienced the conflict firsthand or had relatives who fell victim to Sheridan's torch during the Burning in the autumn of 1864. One female resident of Harrisonburg wrote to her sister in Lynchburg in 1885 about her mixed emotions of seeing these Union veterans again: "The reception of our Yankee friends…could but rouse old memories…we found ourselves again the midst of the bitter struggle, every consideration of policy and courtesy forgotten, and remembering only that we were preparing to meet those who had come before as 'invaders of our sacred soil'…I cannot tell you how I felt as we heard the notes of the 'Star Spangled Banner,' and saw the column but advancing."[227]

As the patriotic song wafted through the air, this same woman noticed her son bending down to pick up pieces of red, white and blue cloth that had accidentally been torn from a U.S. flag and fallen to the ground. The mother asked her son what he was doing. He informed her simply: "I want to keep every piece of our country's flag." This statement shocked the mother, who "felt mingled emotions of pleasure and pain" as her son exhibited "honor and love" to a "flag that was to us the symbol of tyranny and oppression in the wild heat of civil war."[228]

After brief remarks by the association's vice-commander, Elisha Hunt Rhodes, and Harrisonburg's mayor at the train station, the veterans formed a column. The citizens who gazed upon the veterans thought they would march straight to the courthouse for a reception; however, the Union veterans took an unanticipated route and instead marched to the Confederate section of Woodbine Cemetery. As they had done two years before in Winchester,

The train that carried the SVA's members south to Harrisonburg stopped on Narrow Passage Bridge about three miles south of Woodstock. *Author's collection.*

Members of the SVA lay flowers at the base of the monument to the unknown Confederate dead in the Confederate section of Woodbine Cemetery, Harrisonburg. *Author's collection.*

the veterans understood that one of the most useful strategies in furthering their campaign of reconciliation was to engage in outward displays of respect to the Confederate dead.

Sheridan's veterans also understood that in order to successfully advance their campaign of reconciliation in the valley, they needed not only former Confederate soldiers but also Confederate women to accept the war's results and embrace reconciliation. Due to their work with the establishment of Ladies' Confederate Memorial Associations and the construction of Confederate cemeteries, the South's women had emerged as the guardians of Confederate heritage.[229] The ranks of Sheridan's veterans understood that the best method to reconcile with these guardians of the Confederate past was to honor what all former Confederates revered and respected more than anything else—their dead.[230]

Although the impromptu ceremony in Harrisonburg's Confederate cemetery repeated what the veterans had done in Winchester two years prior and had the potential to reap significant rewards for reconciliation, some in the North lambasted the veterans for continuing to show reverence for the Confederate dead. The veterans defended their conduct in the pages of the *Boston Daily Globe:* "No defense is needed of the act. The men who were present were soldiers who had risked life on many battlefields, and if any criticism is offered they do not fear it." Additionally, the association reminded the readers in New England that however reprehensible this action might seem to some in the North, it proved necessary in order to convince former Confederate women to embrace their former foes. "It has always been conceded that the women of the South, who were signally loyal to the cause, have been the most implacable opponents to any steps toward reconciliation, and have been the last to recognize any good as coming from the North."[231]

Sheridan's veterans gathered around the monument in the cemetery's center, which bore an inscription brimming with Lost Cause rhetoric: "Success is not Patriotism. Defeat is not Rebellion." It also offered remarks and prayers for the Confederate dead.[232] General Rhodes delivered the address in the cemetery on behalf of the Union veterans and informed the astonished onlookers that they performed this unannounced activity "in gratitude to a reunited country and to the spirit of reconciliation that now exists between survivors of the Union and Confederate armies, we place these flowers upon the last resting places of your dead, emblematic of that immortality we all hope to attain in the hereafter."[233] "This was entirely unexpected to the citizens," recalled a Harrisonburg resident, "and had a very pleasant effect. On our part, it was the...expression of a sincere respect for the Southern soldier."[234] After the ceremony concluded, the Union veterans received instant feedback as to what Harrisonburg's Confederate women thought of the "brief and touching" display in the cemetery.[235]

A female resident of Harrisonburg dressed in a black mourning dress wanted to test the sincerity of the Union gesture. Although this woman's identity is not known, she had to undoubtedly be a member of Harrisonburg's Ladies' Confederate Memorial Association, which traced its roots back to 1868.[236] The woman asked the Union veterans for financial assistance to help maintain the cemetery. Sheridan's veterans eagerly accepted the request and made a "handsome donation." "Truly our soldiers had met foemen worthy of their steel," the woman stated in an unprepared address to the veterans, "magnanimous men who gave of their means to keep in order the graves of those opposed to them in principles, made impracticable by war, but not wrong."[237] Another female resident of Harrisonburg remarked of the Union veterans' actions: "Could we give greater proof of friendship and fraternity than thus to allow strangers to aid us in caring for our beloved dead? Every eye was dim, and voices grew husky with tender emotion."[238]

For many former Confederates in Harrisonburg, this action, as it had in Winchester's Stonewall Confederate Cemetery two years prior, helped cement the bonds between former foes and pushed others who seemed irreconcilable closer to reconciliation. "After this no bitter thoughts would come. If war stories were told, it was in jest," noted a member of Harrisonburg's Ladies' Confederate Memorial Association. "And as we would exchange experiences of trial and hardship with old friends of whose sympathy we are assured...they have left behind them in the valley of Virginia those who will hold them in loving remembrance. Thus and thus only can wounds be healed...and brethren dwell together in unity."[239]

Following the ceremony at the cemetery and the reception, the veterans gathered that afternoon for the competitive rifle matches. The ground chosen for the competition stood on land owned by Judge John Paul. Paul, himself a Confederate veteran, believed that while the nation could not "afford to forget" the Civil War, it had to move forward and reunite. While Paul did not offer an apology for either side, he informed Rockingham natives and the Union visitors that the Civil War's end was "the best for all people of this land." Additionally, Judge Paul reminded the crowd that although the soldiers of blue and gray might have fought for opposing principles, they had shared experiences that could bring them together. "Today we can meet on common ground, both Union and Confederate, for we shared like toils, like dangers, like victories, and like defeats. We are all American citizens whether with North or South," Judge Paul stated. He concluded his remarks: "Let us join hand and heart in the future to do good to one another, and...do the greatest good to the whole people."[240]

Left: Confederate veteran Judge John Paul. *Seymour Paul private collection.*

Below: A modern-day view of Judge John Paul's farm, where the Blue-Gray Rifle match occurred in 1885. *Seymour Paul private collection.*

The match held on Judge Paul's farm consisted of two teams. Both the Blue and Gray teams had seven members who fired at paper targets at distances of up to five hundred yards. The Gray team outmatched its counterpart. Scores shot by both teams proved anything but remarkable, however. A member of the Blue team recorded: "It will be seen that as between the teams goose-egg honors were easy."[241] Although the Gray team reveled in its success, it did its best to keep the scores a secret. The *Winchester Times* desperately tried to secure the scores for publication but reported that it was "unable to do so."[242]

Although Harrisonburg residents did not witness the finest marksmanship on the afternoon of September 18, they did witness an important act of healing. "It was demonstrated that with proper facilities, easily obtainable, these rifle competitions may be of great value in cementing veteran companionship," one veteran recalled.[243]

As the sun began to set in Harrisonburg, the Union veterans boarded the train cars that would carry them north to Winchester. Both the Union veterans and residents of Harrisonburg reflected positively on the interactions between both sides. "The trip to Harrisonburg was an event never to be forgotten. The hospitality of citizens and military was universally commended, and the Harrisonburg people have reared another 'shaft in memory's hall,'" a Union veteran concluded.[244] A female resident of Harrisonburg who adamantly supported the Confederacy and initially refused any form of forgiveness could not help but change her attitude after she witnessed the gesture of respect at the Confederate cemetery and the interaction among the veterans during the rifle competition. "How different the advent now of these veterans who had helped swell the ranks of Sheridan's army in 1864. They come not with fire and sword, but with countenances beaming with peace and good will and the right hand of fellowship extended to express their willingness to be brothers again; anxious that all should share alike the inheritance due them from our common country," noted the seemingly irreconcilable former Confederate woman.[245]

The day's activities in Harrisonburg caught the attention of media outlets beyond the valley. A reporter from the *Baltimore Sun* believed that the SVA's conduct set the standard for how former enemies could forgive the deeds of the past but not forget the individual sacrifices of men during the conflict and the causes for which they fought. "The best of feeling prevailed throughout, and a good day's work was done toward establishing closer relations between the North and the South," reported the *Baltimore Sun*. "The visitors were profuse in their expression of pleasure at the hospitalities received."[246]

CIVIL WAR LEGACY IN THE SHENANDOAH

When the veterans returned to Winchester that evening, the Vermont veterans of the association held a campfire in honor of their state's service in the Shenandoah. The campfire had become a typical evening activity for the members of the association. One of the characteristic features of the campfire was for veterans of both armies to deliver short speeches that lauded one another's conduct and honor. During the Vermont night campfire on September 18, the Eighth Vermont's Stephen Thomas, who commanded a brigade during Sheridan's Campaign, not only urged national healing but also praised the South's women for the manner in which they encouraged men to enlist in the Confederacy's service. Thomas stated in part: "I am glad that the blue and the gray now meet as friends...During the war I found the women of the South...were more ready to give up their sons, brothers, husbands, fathers, and lovers, buckle on their armor and tell them to go forth and fight bravely...Now...let us not look backward but forward: and if by chance when we speak of valor and bravery in that great contest which is now over forever let us remember that it was all American valor."[247] Captain Joseph Nulton, a veteran of the Stonewall Brigade, reciprocated as he "spoke for the future of his country and pledged that the Confederates would join the veterans of the Union armies to advance all the grand interests of a common country."[248]

Another mainstay of the veterans' campfire was the use of pyrotechnics. These displays not only provided entertainment for the crowd but also sent an important visual message of reconciliation. During Vermont night, the veterans ignited a fireworks display that contained a large figure of a Vermont soldier with his hand extended outward. Arched over the hand were the words "Vermont greets Virginia."[249] During New Hampshire's campfire on the night of September 19, veterans of both armies were treated to a fireworks display that contained an outline of one Union and one Confederate soldier facing each other with clasped hands. At their feet rested the accoutrements of war, and above their heads an arched wreath burned brightly with the word "Fraternity."[250]

The first two full days of the veterans' visit to the Shenandoah Valley focused exclusively on reconciliation; however, as the anniversary date of the Third Battle of Winchester approached, the veterans turned their attention toward honoring the Union veterans who fought and sacrificed at Third Winchester. On the morning of September 19—the battle's twenty-first anniversary—the veterans gathered on the bloody Middle Field where the Eighth Vermont became the manifestation of heroic sacrifice.

During the Third Battle of Winchester, the Eighth Vermont, along with the Twelfth Connecticut, was pinned down and hugged the ground in the bloody Middle Field for around two hours. While their comrades from other Nineteenth Corps units retreated, the soldiers of the Eighth remained and maintained constant fire on the Confederates from General John B. Gordon's division in the Second Woods. On three separate occasions, two sergeants from the Eighth Vermont, Henry Downs and Charles Lamb, rose from the ground and went to the rear to bring additional ammunition to the front line. In 1893, Downs received the Medal of Honor for his actions at Winchester. Lamb, who was mortally wounded at the Battle of Cedar Creek, received none.[251] As if their actions at the Middle Field were not enough, later in the day, the Vermonters followed up their already heroic conduct with a bayonet charge.[252]

The Eighth Vermont's Colonel Herbert E. Hill, who was a private during the Third Battle of Winchester, donated the monument. As the veterans gathered in the Middle Field to dedicate the monument with former Confederates and area civilians, few remarks were made that truly captured the Eighth Vermont's heroism in the battle. Instead of discussing the Vermonters' harrowing experiences, the Union veterans spoke of how the monument commemorated a specific regimental deed and, in doing so, stood as a symbol of the enduring heroism exhibited by both sides during the battle. Colonel John B. Mead, who read Colonel Hill's dedicatory address (Hill was absent because of illness), noted: "The Eighth Vermont, in erecting this monument, knows to-day no North, no South. This shaft speaks to American valor…and while the heroic action of a Vermont regiment is designated, the Confederate veteran may proudly point to this very spot as proving his own bravery and heroism in contending in a hand-to-hand conflict, an American himself, with an American."[253]

Captain Nulton, a veteran of the Stonewall Brigade, accepted responsibility for caring for the monument. He promised the veterans that it "should stand as safely among the hills of Vermont" and that Virginians "would never allow a single letter to be effaced on its pure white surface." Although the monument still survives today, it does not rest in its original location.[254] Ten years after the monument's dedication, the Vermont Quartermaster General's Office requested the monument be relocated to the Vermont section of the Winchester National Cemetery. The State of Vermont contended, and rightfully so, that in its original location on the battlefield, the marble shaft stood "unprotected and uncared for."[255]

After the monument dedication, the veterans spent some time touring the battlefield and then returned to Camp Russell for additional ceremonies. During the keynote address delivered by Charles Coffin, the SVA tested the

The monument to the Eighth Vermont Infantry as it stands today in the Winchester National Cemetery. *Photograph by author.*

limits of reconciliation. Veterans on both sides fully understood that what allowed reconciliation to move forward was a refusal to address any of the conflict's more controversial aspects, such as the constitutionality of secession, slavery's role in the conflict or the treatment of prisoners of war. Coffin, however, attempted to partially break that pattern when he addressed the crowd of thousands. He began his remarks with typical rhetoric of reconciliation, but then he dropped a bombshell on the audience as he began to discuss slavery's role in the coming of secession and, in turn, the conflict. Coffin contended that slavery's existence and the difference in labor systems between North and South made the Civil War inevitable. "In the South labor was regarded as degrading. Slavery made it so. In the North there was dignity in labor. There was character and independence. From the outset the great planters of South Carolina had no great liking to our form of government. They were aristocratic....Free labor, untrammeled for the first time in the history of the world, had exhibited its mighty power, its dignity and majesty," Coffin told the onlookers.[256]

Coffin's remarks are somewhat baffling, as he knew they might slow or halt altogether any further efforts of reconciliation between Sheridan's veterans and former Confederates in the Shenandoah Valley but made them anyway. Although some might view his comments as threatening to postwar healing, the mere fact that he made them and came out unscathed perhaps proves to a degree that some, at least in the Shenandoah Valley, understood slavery's role in secession and the Civil War or, at the very least, were open-minded enough to listen. Additionally, Coffin's statement partially illustrates that the SVA's members felt comfortable enough with their former enemies and had enough faith in their work of reconciliation to make a statement that at a different time and place might have been incendiary. Indeed, as one Union veteran reflected in 1885: "One of the most noticeable features of the excursion was the absence of that feeling of shyness experienced during the first visit to the Valley. There was not so much treading on eggs. We realized that the Confederate soldiers could discuss the war in a more impersonal manner—more in the light that history would regard it. Consequently, there was less restraint in our intercourse, with perhaps a little less of the bloom of romance."[257]

Despite the fact that there were no reported instances of ill will among former Confederates to the Union veterans throughout the remainder of their stay, some members of the association did feel as if they were "treading on eggs" in the immediate aftermath of Coffin's speech. That evening, Union and Confederate veterans gathered at Camp Russell for the formal presentation of the trophy (a solid silver cannon with a gold barrel) to the victors of the Blue-Gray match in Harrisonburg, the Gray rifle team. Colonel Wright presented the trophy to Captain Nulton, but Wright made certain that he handed it to Nulton in a way that did not point the muzzle at Nulton or any members of the audience.[258]

If Colonel Wright or other members of the association believed that Coffin might have offended some former Confederates, they had a prime opportunity to quickly mend some fences the following day. The association set aside Sunday, September 20, for church, a brief dedication of the Thirty-eighth Massachusetts monument in the National Cemetery and the now traditional prayers and strewing of flowers in the Stonewall Confederate Cemetery.

During his remarks in the Stonewall Cemetery, Colonel Wright praised the Confederate dead. The *Winchester Times*, which stated the ceremony "was like apples of gold to pictures of silver," reported that Wright delivered "the testimony of a brave man to dead heroes, who, as he said, died in the cause which they conscientiously felt to be right."[259] Following Wright's speech and prayers, the veterans placed flowers around the mound of the monument to the unknown. Once the veterans performed their now customary act in the Confederate cemetery, Colonel Wright called for Mayor Williams of Winchester to join him at the base of the unknown monument. Wright presented the mayor with a "beautiful gold clasp with words 'Blue—Union—Gray' upon it." This gesture touched Mayor Williams, who "accepted in fitting terms saying that by this piece of strategy we are captured, and in behalf of the Vets of the Southern army we accept this beautiful souvenir and gracefully surrender."[260]

Although this scene had been witnessed two years earlier in Winchester and three days prior in Harrisonburg, the scene of Union veterans in veneration of Confederate dead once again proved emotional. One observer recalled: "Many a silent tear was noticed coursing down the rugged cheeks of veterans of both armies and of the fair ones who stood on this hallowed ground. It is such scenes and incidents as these that go to make the whole world akin." A reporter for the *Winchester Times* believed that actions such as these not only improved the relations among former enemies but also "steeled the souls of those who participated with God in Heaven. Indeed, no one present of blue or gray [went] out…[without] feeling as if it was good to have been there and [thinking] that if the veil could have been rent that the recording angel above could have seen writing approving words against the names of the participants."[261]

On the following day, the Union veterans made their way to Fisher's Hill and Cedar Creek. At Fisher's Hill—a spot that, in the estimation of one veteran, "presents one of the most picturesque views to be found in the Valley"—the veterans toured the battlefield from the area of Crook's flank attack to the defenses of Gordon's division that towered above the Valley Pike. After touring Fisher's Hill, the veterans made their way to Cedar Creek.[262]

While most of the veterans took the train to Fisher's Hill and Cedar Creek, some members of the association decided to reenact Cedar Creek's

Members of the SVA touring the position held by General John B. Gordon's division during the Battle of Fisher's Hill. *Author's collection.*

most storied episode—Sheridan's Ride. Eleven individuals rented horses in Winchester and started their re-creation of the ride from the Logan mansion in Winchester—the same location where Sheridan began his ride to immortality twenty-one years earlier. Described by one of the riders as a "novel episode," the ride made its way to Middletown, where the riders arrived piecemeal. Francis Buffum, a member of the party, described the re-created ride simply: "It was a jolly ride, and some of the valiant knights got left—behind."[263]

Once all the members of the association arrived in Middletown on the afternoon of September 21, they made their way to the wooded ridge on the east side of the Valley Pike to dedicate a monument to the Eighth Vermont—a spot on the battlefield that arguably witnessed more severe fighting and carnage than any other. As part of Colonel Stephen Thomas's brigade, the Eighth Vermont had been asked to do the unthinkable at Cedar Creek—fend off Early's assault to allow General William Emory's Nineteenth Corps sufficient time to readjust its lines to meet the onslaught. The Eighth Vermont, already bloodied from its action at the Third Battle of Winchester one month earlier, took 159 men into the fight at Cedar Creek.

In around thirty minutes, the Vermonters lost 106 men, including 13 of its 16 officers. Colonel Thomas received the Medal of Honor in 1892 for his conduct in defending that ridge.[264]

While the monument, a gift of the regiment's Colonel Herbert E. Hill, contained no fanciful bronze statues or ornate carvings, the Vermonters believed their simple monument adequately symbolized their regiment's experience that morning. "In design it is most appropriate—a massive block of marble, standing on the ground without base or adjunct of any kind, rough on three sides but smoothed on the fourth for the inscription," recalled a Vermonter. Again, as had been the case during the Eighth Vermont monument dedication in Winchester, Colonel Hill could not be present to deliver his address. Instead, it was read by another man present, this time the Eighth Vermont's Captain S.E. Howard. The dedicatory address informed the crowd of Union and Confederate veterans who fought at Cedar Creek that the monument's three rough sides represented three important elements of the Eighth Vermont's service on that ridge during the morning of October 19, 1864. First, each of the three rough sides symbolized the three regimental standard bearers "who were shot down in the terrible hand-to-hand conflict and who died." Second, the three roughs sides served as a reminder that at one point during the fight, the regiment took enemy fire from three directions—front and both flanks. Last, the three rough sides denoted the nearly three-fourths of the regiment who became casualties at Cedar Creek.[265]

Beyond the monument's symbolic meaning, it also served as yet another emblem of reconciliation in the Shenandoah Valley. Captain S.E. Howard, who had been wounded on that spot, informed the onlookers that the veterans of the Eighth Vermont placed the marble stone not merely to commemorate the tremendous human sacrifice suffered by the Vermonters but also to serve as a "pillar stone which shall forever mark an era of genuine fraternal feeling between *us*. Let it be an everlasting covenant that we will not pass over this stone to thee, and thou shalt pass over this pillar to us, for harm."[266] "Let loyalty and fraternity everywhere prevail, and all the social and moral virtues have a high rating with us as a people," noted another veteran during the dedication. "Then will there be ground for the hope that the future of our beloved country may be worthy of its glorious past."[267]

In addition to strengthening the bond between former foes, in the eyes of at least one Vermonter, the Eighth Vermont monument dedication served another purpose—education for future generations who visit the battlefield. One of the regiment's veterans believed the monument would help future

The monument to the Eighth Vermont on the Cedar Creek battlefield. *Photograph by author.*

visitors understand the battle and the cost of human sacrifice. "These places are already enshrined upon the page of history, but their identity is in no way indicated to the stranger visiting these fields. It is one of the objects, and will, I hope, be one of the results of this visit to more certainly ascertain and designate the exact points in the ebb and flow of the tide of battle as it swept over these ridges and along these hillsides."[268]

Following the Eighth Vermont monument dedication, veterans of the Fourteenth New Hampshire visited an impromptu memorial erected in 1881 by regimental historian Francis Buffum along the Nineteenth Corps' trench line. Buffum visited the valley in 1881 while doing research for the regimental history and determined to mark the spot where the Fourteenth

New Hampshire positioned itself at the outset of the battle. Four years later, Buffum and a contingent of the regiment's veterans determined to mark the spot more suitably. When the veterans reached the spot along the Nineteenth Corps' earthworks just north of Cedar Creek, they discovered that it had not been disturbed and inside remained "one of Sutler Farr's dilapidated fruit cans," which contained a handwritten message of Francis Buffum that was "entirely legible." After the veterans determined to mark the spot more durably, five individuals, including Buffum, took off their coats and stacked stones over the original pile of stones. "The original pile was enclosed in a monument well laid up, about three feet base and five feet high." Although the veterans decided to mark the spot more permanently in the future, the feat was never accomplished. The reasons for this are still unclear.[269]

One of the other mysteries is the fate of the makeshift New Hampshire monument. When the New Hampshire veterans departed the valley in 1885, they apparently had a verbal agreement with Belle Grove's owner, James Smellie, "to secure its preservation" and to care for a memorial plaque that would later be installed at the site.[270] Although the monument no longer stands and no plaque is to be found near the regiment's position along the Nineteenth Corps' trench line, it is still plausible that remnants of the Fourteenth New Hampshire's impromptu monument remain. In a study performed by James Madison University in 2006, a substantial pile of stones near the Nineteenth Corps' trench lines was discovered and identified as "an apparent chimney hearth and footer that is rectangular in shape and made of cut limestone blocks put in place with no evidence of mortar." While this may indeed be a chimney, its location and temporary construction make it reasonable to surmise that this, in fact, might be the remnant of the Fourteenth New Hampshire's makeshift memorial.[271]

While the veterans from New Hampshire built their monument, the entire Cedar Creek battlefield bustled with activity as Union and Confederate veterans visited the sites and reminisced. Veterans of both armies "walked side by side, if not arm in arm...and these men who then thought of themselves enemies now meet as friends," recalled one veteran. Another noted of the scene in 1885: "Horseman are galloping from point to point, an interested group is over inspecting the Vermont monument; veterans and ladies are roaming up and down the pike; Sixth Corps men are reconnoitering their old position; the Nineteenth Corps breastworks and the rolling plain are dotted with excursionists."[272]

After touring the battlefield, the veterans gathered at Belle Grove for dinner. Around 5:00 p.m., the veterans boarded the train cars that

Members of the SVA gather on the steps of the Belle Grove mansion, the headquarters of the Army of the Shenandoah during the Battle of Cedar Creek. *Author's collection.*

carried them back to Winchester. Among all the veterans' activities in the Shenandoah Valley in 1885, the monument dedications at Cedar Creek and the touring of the battlefield with former enemies seemed to have left the most lasting impression. One veteran recalled simply of the visit to Cedar Creek: "It was one of the most profitable days of the excursion, and was thoroughly enjoyed."[273]

On the following morning, Tuesday, September 22, 1885, the SVA bid farewell to Winchester and the Shenandoah Valley. The veterans "left Winchester with the kindest of greetings and parting from a crowd of friends."[274] Although this turned out to be the SVA's final visit to the Shenandoah Valley—due, in large part, to financial reasons as well as a weakening of the organization—individual regimental associations whose veterans fought with Sheridan in the valley continued to make visits to the region well into the early 1900s, frequently using Winchester as the base for their gatherings.

As the train cars steamed out of the Shenandoah Valley toward Washington, D.C., that Tuesday morning, the third campaign of Sheridan's veterans in the valley had come to its end. As had been the case two years before, both the residents of the Shenandoah Valley and Sheridan's veterans believed the excursion to be a success. During the train ride to New England, Colonel J.B. Mead—a veteran of the Eighth Vermont—urged his comrades to take news of their positive experiences in the Shenandoah Valley to all they knew, for he understood that reconciliation worked both ways. It took forgiveness not only on the part of former Confederates but also on those in the North as well. Reverend C.H. Kimball from New Hampshire echoed Mead's sentiments. Kimball urged the association members to "carry home to their comrades and families the good news concerning the treatment in the valley, and that the people of Virginia, especially, the old Confederate soldier, had buried the past and were looking toward morning."[275]

Chapter 4

"RECONCILIATION...
A COMMON INTEREST"

The year after the SVA's second visit to the Shenandoah Valley, it organized a gathering in Winchester, New Hampshire. In an attempt to reciprocate the valley's hospitality and further cement the bonds of Union, the SVA's leadership invited Confederate veterans from the Shenandoah Valley to join the SVA in New Hampshire for a three-day reunion held on the twenty-second anniversary of the Third Battle of Winchester. Although accurate rosters do not exist detailing who or how many individuals journeyed from the Old Dominion, evidence indicates that the SVA reunion did have a Confederate presence. The *Boston Daily Globe* reported on September 21, 1886, that the SVA's members had "the opportunity to welcome upon their native hearth men from the South and show them that amid the rocks and hills of New Hampshire hearts can be as warm and hospitality as genuine under the warmer sun and more genial climate of the south."[276] Touched by the Union veterans' cordiality, the Confederate veterans, a reporter for the *Globe* observed, "are loud in their praises of the treatment received here and everywhere since coming North."[277] Sheridan's veterans treated their counterparts from the Shenandoah Valley so well that they refused to let them pay for anything. One member of the contingent from the Shenandoah Valley noted that he had "been trying ever since" he arrived in New Hampshire "to spend a cent," and the Union veterans would not permit it.[278]

By the end of the 1886 gathering, veterans of both sides felt adamant that what they had done in 1883, 1885 and 1886 would prove valuable "in

Veterans of the Fourteenth New Hampshire and their spouses gather during the SVA's reunion in Winchester, New Hampshire, 1886. *Author's collection.*

helping bury for all time to come unpleasant memories of that internecine strife" and that there would be a "better idea of a more perfect union inculcated in the hearts of all."[279]

All immediate signs indicated that the trio of reunions had indeed erased much of the bitterness between former foes and even some of the animosity toward General Philip H. Sheridan. Two months after the veterans gathered in New Hampshire, Sheridan—now general in chief of the U.S. Army—accompanied by Senator J. Donald Cameron of Pennsylvania, visited the Shenandoah Valley. Sheridan, the man referred to as "a Ghoul and barn burning villain" by one Shenandoah Valley newspaper after the conflict, arrived in Woodstock on Monday, November 15.[280] The residents of the Shenandoah County community initially seemed astonished at Sheridan's presence. One newspaper correspondent recorded that "Sheridan was a subject of anxious inquiry on the part of the people, who associated his name with the conflagrations that preceded his last march up the valley."[281] Despite the deep-seated hatred toward Sheridan among so many former Confederates in the region, the general and Senator Cameron were, perhaps somewhat to their surprise, "cordially treated everywhere."[282]

Sheridan avoided, as much as possible, discussions of the Civil War in the Shenandoah Valley. Anytime he sensed the conversation might turn toward the conflict, he found ways to change the subject quickly. For example, when Senator Cameron and Sheridan visited the home of Senator Harrison Holt Riddleberger, a former Confederate officer who served as U.S. senator from Virginia at the time, a member of Riddleberger's family called Sheridan's attention to a photograph of the senator in his Confederate uniform. Although an observer noted that Sheridan looked at the photograph "with interest" Sheridan seemed uncomfortable and looked for an escape from the impending conversation about the conflict. When the senator's three-year-old son, Harry Heath Riddleberger, entered the room, Sheridan changed the topic quickly and informed Senator Riddleberger that "he knew all about babies" and wished to talk about children instead of the war.[283]

Even when Sheridan and Cameron were "appropriately" greeted at the Shenandoah House, the place where they lodged for the evening, Sheridan avoided speaking and instead "deputized to Senator Cameron the duty of acknowledging" the warm welcome.[284]

Less than one year after Sheridan's visit, former Union general William Averell, a man whose career as a cavalry officer in the Union army had been ended by Sheridan in the aftermath of the Battle of Fisher's Hill, visited Staunton, Virginia, to participate with Governor Fitzhugh Lee, a former cavalry foe in the Shenandoah Valley, in a joint memorial ceremony to honor the memory of soldiers "Blue and Gray." During his remarks, Governor Lee turned to Averell and told him "your presence here under these happy auspices clearly indicates that we are in the dawn of revived national feeling, and that we now have peace that is disturbed by no cannons, save those fired in memory of the brave and honored soldiers who fell in both armies." During his remarks, General Averell informed the crowd that he and many of his men felt great regret for what they had done during Sheridan's 1864 Shenandoah Campaign in bringing war against the civilian population. He noted that it was difficult for him to see "women come out of their gates with white faces and disheveled hair" pleading with the Union troopers to protect them and not destroy their property.[285]

The decorations for the memorial service also embodied a sentiment of reconciliation. Special arches of evergreen that spanned Staunton's Main Street and decorated the front of city hall had the words "Our honored dead—Blue and Gray" emblazoned on them. A correspondent for the *Staunton Spectator* found the arches "beautifully appropriate, and sacred in the affections of all hearts."[286]

The following year, when the veterans of the Third Massachusetts Cavalry arrived in Winchester to dedicate a monument to their regiment's

The monument to the Third Massachusetts Cavalry in the Winchester National Cemetery. *Photograph by author.*

service during Sheridan's 1864 Shenandoah Campaign in the National Cemetery, reconciliation's spirit seemed alive and well. As had now become the custom, Winchester's inhabitants, including scores of Confederate veterans, greeted the Massachusetts veterans with open arms. A veteran of the Third Massachusetts noted simply: "The Northern veterans were received most cordially by the Southern ex-Confederates, and citizens generally."[287]

On September 19—the twenty-fourth anniversary of the first great victory of Sheridan's 1864 Shenandoah Campaign—the Massachusetts veterans gathered in the Winchester National Cemetery to dedicate their monument.

After the monument's dedication, the veterans, as had now become customary any time Union veterans visited the region, marched across the street to the Stonewall Confederate Cemetery. The veterans, accompanied by Winchester's Mulligan GAR post under command of E.M. Houston, gathered around the monument to the unknown Confederate dead, offered prayers and then "deposited flowers and wreaths upon the graves."[288]

Before the veterans of the Third Massachusetts departed the region, they presented the gift of a Remington Hepburn target rifle to members of Winchester's Gray rifle team—men whom the Union veterans competed against in the Blue-Gray match three years earlier. The rifle included a German silver–engraved plaque on its butt stock that showed a Union and Confederate soldier standing shoulder to shoulder, one-time enemies now comrades of a united nation.[289]

After a delightful several days in the Shenandoah Valley, the Union veterans returned home. As had been the case in previous visits, the Union veterans reflected positively on their experience. A Winchester newspaper reported: "The Veterans…were delighted with their treatment and profuse in complimentary allusions to our magnificent Valley." Winchester's former Confederates gave them every "assurance" that should they return to the Shenandoah Valley, they would receive "a hearty welcome."[290]

While it seemed that many in the Shenandoah Valley embraced the spirit of reconciliation, the whole notion of fraternization among former foes greatly angered one particular Confederate veteran—Sheridan's ultimate nemesis in the Shenandoah Valley, General Jubal A. Early.

As one of the architects of the Lost Cause, Early became one of the most vociferous defenders of the Confederacy and an obstructionist of postwar reconciliation after the conflict. Usually dressed in a suit of Confederate gray, replete with Confederate flag cuff links, Early loathed the idea of making amends with Union veterans and advancing national healing. Simply put, Early proved to be, in the estimation of historian Gaines M. Foster, "the prototypical unreconstructed Rebel."[291]

The year after the Third Massachusetts Cavalry came to Winchester, Early came to Winchester as the keynote speaker for Confederate Memorial Day services in the Stonewall Confederate Cemetery on June 6. In addition to using his remarks to lambast the reputation of General Sheridan and thank the women of the South for their work in memorializing the Confederate dead, he took that time to berate the Shenandoah Valley's Confederate veterans for extending a hand of reconciliation to Sheridan's veterans in 1883 and 1885. Early believed those Confederate veterans who welcomed

General Jubal Early. *From* Battles & Leaders.

Union veterans in previous years had deserted the Confederate cause. "Again I say," Early informed the onlookers, "the confederate who has deserted since the war is infinitely worse than the one who deserted during the war, for the former has gone over to the enemy at no personal risk to himself and simply from motives of gain, while the latter's life was in his hands, knowing he would be shot if captured, and in a number of cases he was tempted to leave the service to go to the assistance of his family, which he was induced, to believe was starving at home."[292]

For some, Early's blunt comments proved refreshing. One Shenandoah Valley newspaper correspondent noted that Early "spoke his honest sentiments, and for this feature if for no other he has been greatly praised." The journalist even went so far as to suggest that Early's condemnation of Confederates who embraced reconciliation was a "sentiment" that "has been applauded universally."[293]

Early's comments "attracted considerable attention" not only in the Shenandoah Valley but also beyond its borders. A journalist for a newspaper in Wichita, Kansas, headlined his piece about Early's Confederate Memorial Day speech "Unreconstructed." "Old Jubal Early," the correspondent penned angrily, "whose condition is generally described as 'fuller'n-a-biled owl,' managed to get sober enough, on the 6th to make a speech." While the correspondent believed that comments from the "old Blatherskite" Early would be praised "in the hearts of some people in the south," the reporter for the *Wichita Daily Eagle* refused to believe that a majority of Confederate veterans in the Shenandoah Valley, especially those who fought in Early's losing effort in the autumn of 1864, would support his anti-reconciliation message. The reporter opined: "We dare say none of the men who were under him on the memorable occasion referred to [Sheridan's 1864 Shenandoah Campaign] are among the number" who supported Early's message.[294]

Although "numbers of old soldiers, and many citizens paid their respects" to General Early, it appears that his message did little to curb the reconciliation activities of the Shenandoah Valley's citizens.[295]

Around two months after Early's incendiary speech, a contingent of residents from Winchester led by Mayor William Atkinson and the city's Union Cornet Band trekked north to Lynn, Massachusetts, to participate in a reunion of the Third Massachusetts Cavalry. During the gathering, Mayor Atkinson assured the Union veterans that inhabitants of Winchester would do everything in their power to make certain that the graves of Union soldiers would always be properly cared for and honored by the city's inhabitants. Atkinson, recorded a reporter for the *Boston Journal*, "desired to assure the people of Massachusetts, whose sons sleep in that beautiful cemetery in the Valley of the Shenandoah, that their graves should ever receive the care and veneration of his people." The mayor also encouraged the Union veterans to return to the Shenandoah Valley and erect additional monuments. One observer noted that the contingent from Winchester "desired that more of the monuments to the brave Northern dead should be erected in their midst, representing as they did, the bravery, the devotion and the chivalry of the American soldier.[296]

Even former Confederate officers who served on Early's staff during the 1864 Shenandoah Campaign and called the valley home refused to heed his advice to avoid reconciliation, chief among them Jedediah Hotchkiss. For example, when the veterans of the 114th New York visited the Shenandoah Valley in 1894, Hotchkiss spoke to the Union veterans about the Third Battle of Winchester, guided them over the battlefield and participated, along with other Confederate veterans, in a banquet held in city hall. During the banquet, the New Yorkers toasted the Confederate veterans present: "May his Manly Virtues, his Soldierly Qualities, his Fidelity to his Cause and his Prowess in Arms be ever a perpetual Remembrance, and may his Loyalty and his Patriotism and his Fidelity to the Union never again [be] questioned." After the toast and a rendition of "Dixie," Hotchkiss responded to the tribute and thanked the Union veterans.[297]

While Early's comment about "the Confederate who has deserted since the war" did not seem to slow attempts to reconcile North and South, one of his comments might have been taken more seriously—that Confederate veterans should be proud of their past as Confederate soldiers and never do anything to forget their service, the sacrifices of their fallen comrades or the memory of the Confederacy's leaders. Early counseled those in attendance at the Confederate Memorial Day ceremony in 1889 to "never repudiate, disown or apologize for the cause which Lee fought and Jackson died."[298]

Early's statements came in the same year that Confederate veterans established the national United Confederate Veterans in New Orleans, Louisiana. The Shenandoah Valley's Confederate veterans, as well as Confederate veterans throughout the nation, believed that simultaneous efforts could be undertaken to further ameliorate relations with Union veterans while protecting their Confederate past.[299] For example, the members of Winchester's Turner Ashby Camp, No. 22, passed a resolution on September 2, 1895, condemning the use of *A Brief History of the United States* published by one of the largest textbook publishers in the United States at the time, A.S. Barnes & Company. Confederate veteran Francis Edward

Conrad, who served in Captain R. Preston Chew's Artillery Battery during the Civil War, made a motion that condemned the book for "its false history and certain conclusions," believing it "unfit to be put in the hands of the children of our City." Undoubtedly one of the things Conrad and other members of the camp protested in *A Brief History* was the characterization of General Philip H. Sheridan's 1864 Shenandoah Campaign as "the most brilliant of the war" while portraying Early's Confederates as a disorganized mass "routed" by Sheridan's command.[300] Conrad's resolution urged the Winchester school board to "substitute some other history in its place" and that a special committee composed of three members from the Ashby Camp consult with the school board to find an appropriate replacement.[301]

Three weeks later, Turner Ashby Camp veterans again offered another resolution, this time in condemnation of the remarks of Vermont governor Urban A. Woodbury made on September 20, 1895, at the dedication of the Chattanooga, Tennessee portion of Chickamauga-Chattanooga National Military Park. Although the park was established with the intent of being a memorial to postwar reconciliation, the commemorative addresses uttered that day did little to bury the past. After Alabama governor William C. Oates, also a Confederate veteran, made some rather inflammatory remarks about the Civil War's origins, Governor Woodbury now had his opportunity

Members of the Turner Ashby Camp of Confederate Veterans in the 1890s. *Winchester-Frederick County Historical Society/Stewart Bell Jr. Archives, Handley Regional Library.*

to stand behind the podium and chastise the Confederate cause. Woodbury informed the crowd that "the rebellion" was "wrong, and taught his children that those who engaged in it were also wrong."[302]

Angered over Woodbury's remarks, Winchester's Confederate veterans issued a resolution that censured Woodbury for telling "the Southern people that they must teach their children that they were wrong in the recent war." The veterans also thanked Tennessee governor Peter Turney for standing up to Woodbury at the dedication. "That the thanks of this Camp are hereby extended to the Governor of Tennessee for his timely and manly protest against advise [sic] which was certainly unasked for and will be unheeded," the Ashby Camp resolution stated in part. Interestingly the resolution that condemned Woodbury, praised Turney and reiterated the veterans' continued efforts to teach their children about the greatness of Robert E. Lee, Stonewall Jackson and Turner Ashby also stated that the Confederate veterans recognized the United States as "an indissoluble union of indestructible States," one that the veterans attested they "shall bear true allegiance."[303]

After a month of issuing resolutions condemning attacks on the rightness of the Confederate cause, members of the Ashby Camp welcomed veterans of the Eighteenth Connecticut to Winchester on October 9 for the dedication of their regimental monument in the Winchester National Cemetery.[304]

The following year, on the eve of the presidential election of 1896, which pitted William McKinley against William Jennings Bryan, around one thousand Confederate veterans from the Shenandoah Valley made "a pilgrimage" to Canton, Ohio, to show their support for McKinley, a man who served as an officer in Sheridan's Army of the Shenandoah in 1864. Wearing badges that bore the words "No North-no South; no East-No West; the Union forever," the Confederate veterans from the Shenandoah rallied with hundreds of Union veterans in front of McKinley's home in Canton. As a local band escorted the group of veterans to McKinley's residence, playing such familiar tunes as "Dixie" and "Marching through Georgia," crowds lined the streets. When they reached McKinley's home, he welcomed the "men of the Shenandoah Valley" and informed them in part: "We are a re-united country. We have but one flag, the glorious stars and stripes, which all of us love so well…Sectionalism surrendered at Appomattox and the years that followed removed whatever lingering resistance there remained."[305]

For Republican candidate McKinley, the presence of such a large contingent of Confederate veterans from the Shenandoah Valley, despite those same veterans' efforts to protect their heritage and condemn those who blasphemed the Confederate cause, proved that reconciliation was real. McKinley concluded:

> *No stronger evidences, no other testimony is required to prove that sectional lines are obliterated and that war has long been over, than the presence in Canton today of this large assembly of ex-Confederate soldiers, travelling from the Valley of the Shenandoah in Virginia, which marked the bloody pathway of war, to testify their devotion to unbroken and never-to-be-broken Union, and their purpose to uphold its credit and honor forever.*[306]

While the embrace of reconciliation among the Shenandoah Valley's Confederate veterans certainly had its obstacles, it appeared that by 1896, more former Confederates favored burying animosities more than ever before. Less than one month after Confederate veterans from the Shenandoah Valley made their trip to Canton, the Turner Ashby United Confederate Veterans Camp from its post in Winchester issued a bulletin to "Confederate Veterans of the Valley." While the circular reiterated the veterans' position to use "all means in our power to collect and preserve *facts* for the use of the historian and writer" in an effort to safeguard the Confederate past, it also urged all of its members and veterans in the Shenandoah Valley to harbor no animosities toward Union veterans.[307]

Issued as part of a larger directive from the Grand Camp of Virginia, the bulletin informed current and prospective members "not to prolong the animosities, engendered by the war, but to extend to our late adversaries, on every fitting occasion, courtesies which are always proper between soldiers, and which, in our

One of the ribbons worn by Confederate veterans during their visit to Canton, Ohio, in 1896. *Harrisonburg-Rockingham Historical Society, Dayton.*

case, a common citizenship demands at our hands...we will lend our aid to the maintenance of law and the preservation of order."[308]

Not only did Confederate veterans receive encouragement to embrace reconciliation, some attempted to address the issue of what stood as the root cause of the conflict—slavery. While eminent scholars of Civil War memory, most notably David Blight, contend that by the late 1890s the issue of slavery "faded from national consciousness," the Shenandoah Valley offers at least one example of a Confederate veteran in the late 1890s not afraid to address slavery's role in the coming of the conflict.[309] Speaking at the anniversary commemoration of the Battle of New Market on May 15, 1897, Confederate veteran F.R. Farrar admitted to the crowd that the "slavery question may have been the most direct cause of the struggle."[310] Regardless of what people viewed as the Civil War's origins, Farrar encouraged those in attendance, just as the Ashby Camp bulletin urged the previous year, to bury animosities so "that all the issues that antagonized our people may be forever at rest."[311]

Although years of interactions between Union and Confederate veterans advanced healing among former enemies, nothing helped strengthen that bond among veterans and garner a greater sense of allegiance among Confederate veterans to the United States than the Spanish-American War. Around one month after the explosion of the USS *Maine* in Havana Harbor, the Shenandoah Valley's Confederate veterans offered their support to the McKinley administration, as had been the case throughout much of the country. Veterans of Winchester's Ashby Camp unanimously moved on March 21, 1898, that "the General Turner Ashby Camp of 150 veterans, *offer their services* to the United States Government in case of war between the United States and Spain."[312]

While this contingent of Confederate veterans offered their services to the federal government, a debate ensued about whether or not the camp should begin to carry the U.S. flag. Some former Confederates believed in early October 1898, two months after American victory over the Spanish in Cuba, that the time had arrived for Confederate veterans to begin unfurling the Stars and Stripes at all functions. Two members of the camp disagreed and contended that they should never march under the banner that had stood against the Confederacy.[313]

Two weeks after the Confederate veterans debated the flag's use, they welcomed, for the second time in four years, veterans of the 114th New York. This time, the veterans came not only to visit the battlefields of Sheridan's 1864 Shenandoah Campaign but also to dedicate a regimental monument in the Winchester National Cemetery. As had been the case during previous visits of Union veterans to the Shenandoah Valley, the local inhabitants greeted them warmly. During the official welcome of the New York veterans on the morning of October 19, Winchester's mayor, John J. Williams, informed the Union veterans that he welcomed another monument in the national cemetery, as it would prove instructive to future generations. Williams told the New Yorkers that their monument would undoubtedly help "teach the ingenuous youth to honor the American soldier fighting for conscience sake and to emulate his example. Be it the sacred and solemn duty of ourselves and those who are to come after us, as far as the limitations of human weakness permit and enable it, to see it that the conscience be rightly instructed and wisely directed."[314]

Despite Mayor Williams's warm reception, the 114th captain Charles W. Underhill used the opportunity in his response to Williams's remarks to not merely reciprocate the mayor's kind words but also address an issue that bothered a number of Union veterans—the appropriate use and display of Confederate battle flags. Since the dedication of General Robert E. Lee's equestrian statue in Richmond on May 29, 1890—largely regarded as the first major appearance of Confederate flags since the Civil War's end—Union veterans seemed divided over whether or not Confederate flags should be flown again.[315] Unlike some Union veterans, Underhill believed Confederate flags should be allowed to be displayed at appropriate functions but never be utilized to encourage the government's dissolution or be used to intimidate. To address the issue, one which is still highly debated in society today, Underhill posed a series of questions to the crowd: "But how about our old battle flags? What shall we do with them? And our flag, the flag which waves over our boys today, what shall it contain?" For Underhill the answer seemed simple. He informed the onlookers: "Since the time when civilization first began to make laws for a people, it has never been thought wise to display the emblems of civil strife. The law of preferring one another determines this rule of conduct. The flag is the symbol of sovereignty, and not the record of personal triumph." Underhill believed the flags of both armies should be kept "as mementoes… the rare ornament of our State houses, and arsenals. Yes, let us carry them on rare occasions (they are too precious for every day use), but let it all be done in the spirit of loyalty to country."[316]

While Underhill had no qualms about addressing such a controversial topic during the morning reception at the courthouse, the 114th New York major O.H. Curtis used his keynote address during the monument dedication ceremony in the national cemetery to pay tribute to not only the veterans of the Empire State who fought so fiercely during the battles of Sheridan's 1864 Shenandoah Campaign but the memory of Confederate veterans as well. After citing all the battles in which the 114th took part and the casualties suffered, Curtis informed the Confederate veterans present that "this brief record of the services and sacrifices of the old 114th Regiment bears incontrovertible evidence of your fidelity to your cause, your courage and heroism on the battlefields, and can but add luster to your war record, among your people especially."[317]

Major Curtis hoped that with time, all negative memories of the conflict would fade. "Let us now," Curtis proclaimed, "if we have not before, banish from our memories every element of those deplorable conflicts save that of mutual admiration for each other's conscientious convictions of truth and duty, each other's fidelity to his cause and the courage, bravery and heroism displayed in defending the same upon the battlefields of the war." Despite Curtis's proclaimed desire to live in a state of denial, to "bury every error, cover every defect and extinguish every resentment," he did conclude his address with a statement about the Union fighting for all that was right and the Confederacy fighting for everything that was wrong. "Unquestionably," Curtis stated to the crowd,

The dedication of the 114th New York Monument in the Winchester National Cemetery occurred in 1898. *Author's collection.*

"the truth and right prevailed. Unquestionably, in the final wind up, the nation advanced to a higher level, and a higher civilization."[318]

After the dedicatory services concluded in the national cemetery, the Union veterans again marched to the Stonewall Confederate Cemetery and paid tribute to the Confederate dead by placing flowers at the base of the unknown Confederate soldiers monument. Following that tribute, the 114th's veterans, accompanied by members of Winchester's Turner Ashby Camp and Mulligan GAR post, strewed flowers on every Confederate grave in the cemetery.[319]

The day concluded with a visit by the 114th to the Ashby Camp meeting room and a dinner at the courthouse, a venue that one member of the regiment remarked "was taxed to its utmost capacity, and standing room was at a premium." With a crowd "composed of many veterans of both armies, their families and friends and many ladies and gentlemen of the city," the New Yorkers believed that "good nature prevailed throughout" the evening.[320] As was customary with these types of gatherings, the veterans made a number of toasts. While the veterans toasted the "Union and Confederate Volunteers" as well as "the volunteer soldiers who responded to the call to defend the national honor, uphold our dignity and oppose the iniquitous rule of Spain," perhaps the most poignant toast aimed at reconciliation came when a veteran of the regiment, identified simply as Corporal Tanner, toasted the women of the Confederacy—the guardians of Confederate heritage. One observer recalled that Tanner "paid the women of the South a graceful compliment upon their devotion and unfaltering sense of duty."[321] At least in the estimation of one newspaper correspondent present during the dinner, Tanner's respectful remarks to Confederate women proved "the event of the evening."[322]

As the veterans prepared to depart the Shenandoah Valley the following day, both Shenandoah Valley inhabitants and Union veterans viewed this visit as another positive step toward reconciliation. Major Curtis believed the gathering would prove "the most remarkable re-union ever held by the Association. It was, as it was planned to be, historical and memorable." A correspondent for a Winchester newspaper observed that the events surrounding the 114th New York's visit were "the personification of joviality and sunshiny fun."[323]

As the nineteenth century neared its end, real signs existed in the Shenandoah Valley that nearly two decades' worth of monument dedications, visits by Union veterans and gatherings of those who fought with Sheridan's army in 1864 and their Confederate counterparts had helped ease tensions.

The visits of Union veterans to the Shenandoah not only helped ameliorate relations with Confederate veterans but also aided in erasing animosity in the minds of some of the Shenandoah Valley's residents who suffered significantly during Sheridan's 1864 Shenandoah Campaign. For example, Emma Howard Wright, a correspondent for *Blue & Gray: The Patriotic American Magazine* (a publication that first appeared in 1892 and urged reconciliation), interviewed a resident of Fisher's Hill. Identified simply as "the old farmer" who lived near the base of Little North Mountain, the elderly gentleman informed Wright that for many years after the Civil War, he had held "very bitter feelings in my heart against the North," but after having viewed the veterans' visits to Fisher's Hill and reflecting on the conflict, he told Wright that "these have all died away now. I have grown to look upon it in this light—that they fought, as we did, for what they considered right."[324]

While it appeared at the close of the nineteenth century that significant progress had been made in healing the deep wounds of the Civil War in the Shenandoah Valley, the new century still provided frequent reminders that although advances might have been made and animosities lessened, obstacles still remained on the path of reconciliation.

Chapter 5

"KEEPING THE APPOMATTOX CONTRACT"

In the aftermath of American victory over the Spanish in Cuba, President McKinley embarked on a tour of the South in an effort to build support for the administration's postwar peace program and foray into imperialism.[325] In late May 1899, McKinley visited the Shenandoah Valley as part of his tour. A veteran of Sheridan's 1864 Shenandoah Campaign, President McKinley hoped that American success in the Spanish-American War and his subsequent tour through the South would eliminate any final obstacles to postwar reconciliation. McKinley, who believed that Union and Confederate veterans at the end of the nineteenth century were bound together by "one sentiment—that of loyalty to the Government of the United States, love of our flag and our free institutions"—received a warm welcome at his various stops in the valley.[326] A newspaper correspondent observed that all along the route of McKinley's train, countless numbers greeted McKinley at the railroad stations with "flags...and flowers." To the journalist who witnessed these displays of admiration for McKinley, it seemed that "if there is any bitterness remaining over the civil strife, there was nothing in the enthusiasm shown today to indicate it."[327] When McKinley's train stopped in Strasburg, a Confederate veteran "hobbled" by a wound he received during the Civil War went up to the president and told him that although he was "an old rebel" he desired "to shake hands" with McKinley.[328]

En route to Winchester, McKinley passed through and stopped to tour portions of the battlefields that helped define his legacy as a soldier. When McKinley arrived in Winchester, he visited the graves of some of his

President William McKinley. *Author's collection.*

friends who were killed during Sheridan's 1864 Shenandoah Campaign and buried in the national cemetery. After paying his respects, McKinley crossed the street and "visited the graves of the confederate dead."[329]

McKinley's tour throughout the Shenandoah Valley and the former Confederacy appeared in the estimation of some the crucial step to erasing any remaining vestiges of postwar animosity among former foes. A journalist for the *Philadelphia Inquirer* concluded after McKinley's sojourn through the Shenandoah Valley: "Everywhere the President was received with an enthusiasm that has never been aroused by the presence of any other Republican President in the Southern states." The correspondent optimistically continued: "War has its evils which everybody can perceive, but it has indirect compensations often of the greatest magnitude, which the wisest cannot foresee. The war with Spain has been worth to the United States a thousand times its cost."[330]

Despite the portrayal by newspaper correspondents of McKinley's tour as a major victory for postwar reconciliation—one that McKinley believed would forever erase remaining hatreds—the activities of some Confederate veterans in the Shenandoah Valley as the twentieth century dawned served as a useful reminder that much work still needed to be done to advance reconciliation's cause and that some Confederate veterans would never embrace reconciliation with their Union counterparts.

As the frequency of Confederate veterans' deaths increased, by the early 1900s, there seemed to be a shift among surviving Confederate veterans to do all they could to protect their historical legacy and make certain that they cultivated in their sons and grandsons an affinity for their Confederate heritage. Historian Peter Carmichael asserted of this phenomenon's emergence after the Spanish-American War: "With the passing of every comrade," Confederate veterans "felt a renewed sense of urgency to protect their historical reputations...the enthusiasm younger Southerners expressed for the Spanish-American War...concerned older Confederate veterans, who worried that their military exploits were being forgotten."[331]

At an October 8, 1900 meeting of the Turner Ashby United Confederate Veterans Camp, members passed a scathing resolution in condemnation of a statement that came from a recent Grand Army of the Republic meeting. The statement asserted that history textbooks being utilized in the South not only taught "false history" but also helped inculcate "unpatriotic ideas in the youth of the land." While not the camp's first foray into the history textbook debate, it undoubtedly felt a greater sense of urgency to defend history textbooks that taught "the truth" in schools throughout the South.[332]

In the same year that some of the valley's Confederate veterans lambasted the Grand Army of the Republic, President McKinley ordered dozens of Confederate dead buried around Washington, D.C., to be reinterred in Arlington National Cemetery. While McKinley believed this an important act of reconciliation, some Confederate veterans in the Shenandoah Valley did not approve of Confederate dead buried near Union veterans on land confiscated from General Lee. Confederate veterans from Winchester adopted a resolution in the spring of 1901 that vehemently "protest[ed] that any of our soldiers be interred in Arlington Cemetery."[333]

Regardless of the Shenandoah Valley's Confederate veterans' efforts to more aggressively defend their heritage at the start of the new century, they still embraced the notion of reunion with their Union counterparts. For example, just three years removed from their defense of southern textbooks and condemnation of interment of Confederate dead at Arlington, a contingent of veterans from Frederick County, Virginia, accepted an invitation from veterans of the Fifty-fourth Pennsylvania to journey to Johnstown, Pennsylvania, for a Blue-Gray reunion in October 1904.[334] The reunion with the veterans from the Keystone State continued, in the estimation of one newspaper correspondent, the campaign of reconciliation begun in 1883. The journalist recorded of the reunion's impact: "'The war is over' has been adopted as the watchword of this notable reunion…the men who have felt the fierce thrill of battle—were strengthening…the once almost severed bonds of American citizenship uniting two great sections of the Republic."[335]

Having had a number of positive interactions with the Shenandoah Valley's Confederate veterans over the previous two years, the Fifty-fourth Pennsylvania's veterans hoped that the year following the Blue-Gray reunion in Johnstown, they could return to the Shenandoah Valley to dedicate a monument to the regiment's memory on the New Market Battlefield. With approval from the Pennsylvania state legislature to spend $2,000 on the monument, the veterans journeyed to the Shenandoah Valley in late October 1905 to dedicate the monument, which stood near where the regiment guarded General Franz Sigel's left flank during the battle, one in which General John C. Breckinridge's Confederates bested Sigel's command.[336]

In the months before the monument's dedication, Shenandoah Valley newspapers tracked the progress of the Fifty-fourth Pennsylvania Veterans' Association as it made final preparations for the event. Additionally, some of the region's newspapers tried to promote the event so that Confederate veterans, particularly those who fought at New Market, would attend the dedication scheduled for October 25, 1905. The *Rockingham Register*, a Harrisonburg-based newspaper, implored its Confederate veteran readers: "An invitation will be extended to all ex-Confederate veterans to be present, especially members of the 62nd Va., the VMI cadets, and others who took part in the battle."[337]

While the Pennsylvanians had every reason to believe that they would be welcomed to the Shenandoah Valley with open arms to dedicate a monument to the memory of the nearly 150 men the regiment lost in the battle, a newspaper article penned around two months before the dedication date reminded them that while reconciliation might have taken hold in the Shenandoah Valley with many Confederate veterans, it had not appealed to all. Among those who disparaged the idea of another Union monument in the Shenandoah Valley was Confederate veteran J.E. Hopkins. Hopkins believed the monument "a thorn in the flesh" of the region's inhabitants. Furthermore, Hopkins believed that if the Pennsylvanians wanted to truly do something to advance healing between former foes, they should take the $2,000 appropriation from the Pennsylvania legislature and distribute it to the people of Shenandoah County who suffered some of the worst devastation at the hands of Sheridan's Army of the Shenandoah in the autumn of 1864. "If they are anxious to do something honorable they can pay something on the barns and mills they burned," Hopkins wrote, "the horses and cattle they stole, the grain and property they despoiled this very people of." In his vitriolic rant, Hopkins branded the Pennsylvanians and all Union soldiers who fought in the Shenandoah Valley criminals who "waged" war "on the helpless Southern people."[338]

Despite Hopkins's abrasive remarks about the "deviltry" of Union soldiers in 1864, the monument dedication had scores of Confederate veterans in attendance. Among the Confederate veterans who attended were Shenandoah Valley residents David B. Sites, James H. Dwyer and W.R. Fallis, who fought against the Fifty-fourth Pennsylvania during the battle as part of the Sixty-second Virginia Infantry. A correspondent for a Harrisonburg newspaper noted of the dedication: "In the crowd today were quite a number of old Confederates, many of them in uniform, who took pains to make the visitors feel at home and who aided them in getting their bearings on the battlefield." As had been the case with previous Union monument dedications in the Shenandoah Valley, the Union veterans made it clear that the monument was not placed "as an evidence of exultation over victory, but rather as a tribute to American Valor and Patriotism which had been displayed on both sides of that great conflict."[339]

While the residents of New Market and Confederate veterans greeted the Union veterans with cordiality and respect, the region's inhabitants, especially those who delivered remarks during the day, did not want their warm welcome to the Union veterans to be mistaken as an apology for the Confederacy. For example, after the singing of "America" at the opera house in New Market following the ceremony on the battlefield, C.W. Bennick, speaking on behalf of the community's mayor, spoke to the crowd in such a way as to indicate that although the Confederate armies had been defeated, former Confederates would never apologize for fighting against the Union or

The Fifty-fourth Pennsylvania Infantry monument on New Market battlefield. *Shenandoah Valley Battlefields Foundation, photograph by Terry Heder.*

admit any wrongdoing. A correspondent who covered the day's activities reported that Bennick's remarks were "cordial in tone and complimentary to the visitors without being apologetic in its treatment of the Civil War questions as seen from the Southern standpoint."[340]

Although the venomous words of men such as Hopkins did not elicit a public reaction from Union veterans—or, at least, not one that could be found—some Confederate veterans in the Shenandoah Valley clearly could not tolerate these men who continued to "wave the bloody shirt" in the early twentieth century. Among those who detested the likes of Hopkins was R.D.

Veterans of the Fifteenth New Jersey pose with members of the Stover Camp of Confederate Veterans at Fisher's Hill in May 1907. *Author's collection.*

Funkhouser, commander of the Stover Camp of Confederate Veterans, an organization based in Strasburg, Virginia. When veterans of the Fifteenth New Jersey visited the Fisher's Hill battlefield in May 1907, Funkhouser and the members of his camp welcomed the veterans with "friendly words and with kindly feelings." Aggravated with those who continued to block the spirit of reconciliation in the new century, Funkhouser informed the gathering of 110 Union veterans and their wives, "It affords us pleasure to meet you under our own vine and fig tree...we welcome you most cordially...It is true we had a little unpleasantness in the long ago, but I venture to say that the man who waves the bloody shirt to-day never smelled gun powder even in those days that people were so careless with it."[341]

Undoubtedly pleased with Funkhouser's statement and condemnation of former Confederates who blocked any effort at reconciliation, the veterans of the Fifteenth New Jersey recognized—as did most Union veterans—that it was not only Confederate veterans who "wave the bloody shirt" who needed to be overcome but Confederate women as well. In the conflict's aftermath, Union veterans understood Confederate women's roles in caring for and memorializing the Confederate dead. By the early twentieth century, the daughters and granddaughters of Confederate veterans were viewed as the guardians of all things Confederate. For example, the members of Clarke County's J.E.B. Stuart Camp of Confederate Veterans stated in the early 1900s that they "look with hope and confidence to the organization of the UDC [United Daughters of the Confederacy], to take up and carry on the work of the Camps, when they go out of existence, which must be in a few years." The Stuart Camp, as did most throughout the South, viewed the UDC as that "organization" which "was and is to collect and preserve material for a truthful history of the war between the States."[342]

Keenly aware of all that would be eventually placed on the shoulders of these women and the ways in which women could help advance or hinder reconciliation, the veterans of the Fifteenth New Jersey thanked the members of the UDC who welcomed them at Fisher's Hill. Before the Union veterans departed Fisher's Hill, the Fifteenth's A.W. Whitehead expressed deep gratitude to the UDC. Whitehead told the Stover Camp and UDC members:

> *Now in conclusion and before we say good-bye, we want to thank you for your very kind…hospitality and the manner in which you have received us who were once your enemies, but we hope now and forever to be your fast friends and comrades. Then to the ladies of your camp—The Daughters of the Confederacy—do we extend more than thanks for the generous repast. May they live long to remember this highly appreciated outing.*

As the veterans departed Fisher's Hill for Winchester, Whitehead recalled that the "ladies of the Confederate Camp" serenaded the Union veterans with a rendition of "Dixie," a gesture which Whitehead believed "was a fitting conclusion to the enjoyable hours spent at Fisher's Hill."[343]

Five months after the 15th New Jersey's veterans visited Fisher's Hill, the veterans of the 128th New York Infantry gathered on the Cedar Creek battlefield "to memorialize the men who lost their lives in that engagement" with a granite monument. Confederate veterans from Funkhouser's Stover Camp "came in a body and in uniform to give the [Union] visitors a welcome and fraternal greeting."[344] The dedication not only became a tribute to the heroism of the 128th New York and its Confederate counterparts but also offered a stage to a voice from the postwar generation—attorney Herbert S. Larrick from Winchester, who urged Confederate veterans and their families to live in the present, look to the future and abandon the hatred of the past without forgetting their Confederate heritage.

After dedicatory remarks by New York veteran Derrick Brown that stated the monument "marks the spot where men met men and Americans met Americans…and…will serve the broader and the better purpose

Above: The wives of veterans from the Fifteenth New Jersey gather with members of the United Daughters of the Confederacy at Fisher's Hill in May 1907. *Author's collection.*

Right: The monument to the 128th New York Infantry on the Cedar Creek battlefield. *Photograph by author.*

of memorializing every effort and every sacrifice made upon this soil, hallowed as it is by the blood here shed forty-three years ago," the podium was turned over to Larrick, who spoke on behalf of the Shenandoah Valley's residents.[345]

Larrick, who termed himself part of "a younger generation," posed a question to the crowd—how would Shenandoah Valley residents explain this monument's presence to future travelers who knew nothing of the region's history? For Larrick, the monument proved a useful tool to illustrate the heroism of the American citizen-soldier and a permanent memorial to "two armies composed of brave men and true...[who] met in deadly conflict over a constitutional principle...a question of sovereignty—state or national." Larrick informed the crowd that he would never under any circumstances "offer [an] apology for the position taken by the south on this great constitutional question." Although Larrick refused to apologize for the Confederacy's actions, he did state that while former Confederates hold "the memory of the old south...dear...and to us [although those memories] are sacred, they belong to the past." As part of the postwar generation, Larrick urged those valley residents present to not forget "our sacred history" but to move forward and not inculcate in their children and grandchildren hatred for Union veterans or the national government. He implored the Confederate veterans present to "teach our young men patriotism as you learned it from your fathers...Lastly you should teach our young men that there is no north for the northerner; no south for the southerner, but one grand glorious America for the patriotic and liberty-loving Americans."[346]

Larrick was not alone in his belief that the generation of sons and grandsons of Confederates needed to not forget but move forward. For example, during the annual gathering of veterans at Fisher's Hill in 1909, R. Gray Williams, city solicitor of Winchester and son of Confederate veteran Colonel John J. Williams, delivered remarks that "defined the duties of Sons of Confederate veterans." Williams believed that it should be the role of that organization, to which he proudly belonged, to pledge its "determination to hasten the complete reunion of the sections."[347]

Despite the encouragement from both Confederate veterans and sons of veterans to heal the Civil War's wounds, some former Confederates still nursed hatred toward the Union and took every opportunity they had to make their disdain public. One year after Williams implored the Sons of Confederate Veterans to "hasten the complete reunion of the sections," Confederate veteran Holmes Conrad addressed the gathering at Fisher's Hill. A veteran of General Thomas Rosser's cavalry command during the conflict

Confederate veterans parade through downtown Winchester during Confederate Memorial Day in 1914. *Winchester-Frederick County Historical Society/Stewart Bell, Jr. Archives, Handley Regional Library*.

Conrad seethed bitterly—nearly a half century after Lee's surrender—about the war. When Conrad reached the podium, the Confederate veterans greeted him with the "rebel yell," which, according to a newspaper correspondent, "surprised thousands of the younger generation." Conrad used his speech to "show why Virginia was justified in withdrawing from the Union" and condemn President Abraham Lincoln. From Conrad's perspective, Lincoln did not do nearly enough to avoid the conflict. A journalist recorded of Conrad's remarks: "He said that he wanted young people to know that Virginia did not act hastily or unwisely. She tried to avert war, but he said her purposes were defeated by Mr. Lincoln and public men of the North who loved money more than human life."[348] Despite his incendiary tone, the scores of Union veterans present seemed to shrug off Conrad's remarks. One observer noted: "Many Union veterans were in the throngs, as has been customary since the Fisher's Hill event became a reunion of more than passing notice, and nothing, occurred to mar the pleasure of the day."[349]

Regardless of the anger some Confederate veterans still harbored in the early twentieth century, signs of progress in healing the Civil War's wounds appeared as the United States confronted World War I. As Confederate veterans watched their sons and grandsons go to the killing fields of Europe, they knew that in order to support them they had to support the United States any way they could. Not coincidentally, the Confederate Memorial Day in Winchester in 1917, just two months after President Woodrow Wilson's appeal to Congress for a declaration of war against Germany and its allies, included something never before seen in the Stonewall Confederate Cemetery—an American flag draped over the monument to the unknown Confederate dead.[350]

American entry into World War I not only brought about the presence of the American flag in Stonewall Confederate Cemetery but also prompted many in the Shenandoah Valley to fly the flag from their porches and above doors. Interestingly, however, the American flag flew with the Confederate flag next to it—showing that while American patriotism flourished in 1917, the Shenandoah Valley's former Confederates still clung to their Confederate past. As one chronicler noted at the time: "In 1917 the Valley fought again—the Valley which had been for a generation a home for old soldiers. The streets were brave with flags. For the first time in fifty years the

A parade in Front Royal, Virginia, in 1919 welcomes home the community's World War I veterans. While American flags and patriotic symbols were abundant throughout the Shenandoah Valley by this point, Confederate flags were still displayed (see right side of image) on patriotic occasions such as this one. *Author's collection.*

Stars and Stripes floated above doorways. But at doorway after doorway it was crossed with the Stars and Bars."[351]

The American flag draped over the unknown monument and flying in the valley's communities proved a sign of reconciliation but one about which some Confederate veterans still had mixed emotions. While some Confederate veterans, such as Randolph Barton, believed that Confederate veterans needed to move on with life; "inculcate" in their "children, love of country"; and continue "keeping the Appomattox contract," Barton's belief that the oaths Confederate soldiers took at Appomattox "required" Confederate veterans to "give our whole souled allegiance to the United States, or quit the country"—he still held bitterness toward the national flag. He once informed a crowd during a gathering at the Stonewall Confederate Cemetery: "I must confess that the unfolding of the Stars and Stripes does not thrill me with patriotic feeling. I saw it advance upon my people for the first time in my life, at Manassas. I saw it then the emblem of all that I hated."[352]

While some Confederate veterans undoubtedly held Barton's view of the American flag in the World War I era, others seemed to embrace the flag without any reservation. Confederate veteran Samuel P. Buck, a native of Warren County who served as a captain in the Thirteenth Virginia Infantry during the conflict, had no qualms with the American flag. Although proud of his Confederate past and "ever ready to defend the cause of the South and Confederate soldiers," he still maintained "love for the Stars and Stripes."[353]

The emblem that Barton held bitterness toward had become the banner under which two of his sons fought in World War I. Confronted with the complexity of patriotism in the early twentieth century versus the Confederate past, perhaps Barton summed up the sentiment that many Confederate veterans felt as they juxtaposed their support for the American war effort in Europe, their desire for some degree of national healing with Union veterans and their Confederate past. "There is no difficulty in pursuing an honest life in our relations to the past and the present," Barton informed a crowd in the Stonewall Confederate Cemetery. Believing that the Union veterans did not "require" Confederate veterans to "forget my Confederate people living and dead," Barton stated, "I do not feel bound to say that I am glad the [Civil] war ended as it did…I can forgive it all but simple truth requires me to declare that I cannot forget it."[354]

Despite the misgivings some might have had about the presence of the American flag on the monument to the unknown Confederate dead in the Stonewall Confederate Cemetery, it seems to have become a normal practice throughout the duration of Confederate Memorial Days observed by members of the Ashby Camp. As a further sign of national healing, during the Confederate Memorial Day in 1918, the American flag in the Winchester National Cemetery was lowered to half-staff until noon.[355]

By the end of World War I, countless numbers of Union veterans had visited the Shenandoah Valley, erected monuments and interacted with Confederate veterans, and conversely, countless numbers of Confederate veterans had welcomed Union veterans with open arms, participated in various ceremonies, journeyed north to participate in reunions with former enemies and guided Union veterans over the Shenandoah Valley battlefields that defined their legacies. Additionally, by the early 1900s, Confederate veterans appeared to have no qualms with Union veterans who called the Shenandoah Valley home after the war. For example, Joseph A. Potts, who served in the 203rd Pennsylvania Infantry and after the conflict joined Winchester's Mulligan GAR post, felt welcome in Frederick County, Virginia. Potts recorded that "among the people" of the Shenandoah Valley, despite his service in the Union war effort, "he has no known enemy."[356]

What undoubtedly furthered that spirit of national healing in the Shenandoah Valley in the early twentieth century was the continued respect that Union veterans showed toward the Confederacy, particularly at monument dedications. For example, when the North Carolina Historical Commission and the North Carolina Division of the United Daughters of the Confederacy dedicated a monument to the memory of General Stephen Dodson Ramseur—mortally wounded at the Battle of Cedar Creek—on September 16, 1920, one of the main speakers was a Union veteran, Colonel Henry A. DuPont.[357] A classmate of Ramseur's at West Point, DuPont commanded the Union artillery in General George Crook's corps during the Battle of Cedar Creek and was among a cadre of Union officers who sat by Ramseur's bedside during his final hours at Belle Grove. While DuPont could not have approved of the cause for which his friend fought, his friendship and admiration for Ramseur transcended wartime allegiance. DuPont stated: "As a close friend…I held him in most affectionate remembrance." He praised Ramseur's ability and proclaimed him a "gallant soldier and splendid son of the Old North State."[358]

By the time DuPont spoke at the Ramseur monument dedication in 1920, a time when the ranks of both Union and Confederate veterans had become "greatly thinned," animus in the Shenandoah Valley toward the Civil War's outcome and the Union army had dramatically improved among a seeming majority of the population. By that point, former Confederates in the Shenandoah Valley appeared, in the belief of a resident of Warren County,

The monument to General Stephen Dodson Ramseur on the Cedar Creek battlefield.
Photograph by author.

to have forgiven and forgotten "the rough usages of the war" and taken hold "of the larger views" intended to "strengthen and ennoble the life and influence of our nation."[359]

Despite the great strides made over the half century since the conflict's end to make, in the words of Confederate veteran Robert T. Barton, "many *great* changes in our way of looking at things," some Confederate veterans nursed their hatred until death. Among a seemingly small minority of Confederate veterans who refused to ever reconcile and admit defeat was Confederate veteran George W. Dellinger, a veteran of the Twenty-third Virginia Cavalry.

Identified by the Winchester *Evening Star* as "an unreconstructed Rebel," Dellinger once informed a journalist in 1936, on the eve of his journey as part of a contingent of Confederate veterans to the Antietam battlefield, that "he will never admit that the soldiers of Lee and Jackson were whipped by the Yankees…The Yankees didn't whip us—they starved us."[360]

Dellinger proved the exception rather than the rule in the Shenandoah Valley—especially by the early twentieth century. The words of Confederate veterans in postwar writings, speeches and monument dedications reveal that many embraced some level of healing with their former battlefield foes. Additionally, the largely positive interactions between Union and Confederate veterans in the decades after the conflict serve as testament to the willingness of former foes to move forward.

That desire to heal and move forward came with one caveat, however: neither side would reconcile at the expense of its heritage or sense of right. At least one Union veteran who visited the Shenandoah Valley in 1907 not only defended the Union cause but also boasted about his role commanding a contingent of Union troops responsible for destroying a number of barns and mills during the Burning in late September and early October 1864. When Union veteran William H. Cawley encountered a Confederate veteran who lamented the destruction Sheridan's men brought to the Shenandoah Valley in the autumn of 1864 at Fisher's Hill in 1907, Cawley informed the Confederate veteran that he was "especially efficient in burning mills and destroying mills" and that his command did "their work well."[361]

After decades of interactions in the Shenandoah Valley among veterans of opposing armies, the fact still remained that while relations had dramatically improved between former enemies, neither Union nor Confederate veterans wished to abandon their perspective of the war. Gray Williams, a member of Winchester's Sons of Confederate Veterans Camp who spoke to a contingent of Union veterans from the Fifteenth New Jersey Infantry in

1907, perhaps best captured the desire of veterans of both sides and their descendants to preserve their view of the conflict for themselves and future generations while simultaneously embracing respect for their wartime foe. Williams "expressed the belief that there was never a higher, nobler or more splendid civilization than that which flowered under the Slavery regime before the War, and withered before the fierce blasts of battle." Despite Williams's positive perspective on that institution that President Lincoln admitted was "somehow, the cause of the war"—a conflict that claimed the lives of nearly 750,000 people—he conveyed the desire of the Shenandoah Valley's Confederate veterans and their descendants to embrace those who fought in a war that preserved the Union and destroyed slavery.[362] Williams informed the New Jersey veterans that "he was ready to welcome as friends and fellow citizens of a united country the men who fought a good fight in the North, and it is good that you come here…with observant eyes that you may better understand us and enable us the better to know you."[363]

Epilogue
"HOPE FOR THE FUTURE"

When the Sheridan's Veterans' Association visited the Shenandoah Valley for the second time in 1885, former Confederate general Fitzhugh Lee believed that the interactions between veterans of the Army of the Shenandoah and those who fought under General Early's command in the autumn of 1864 would "result in producing fraternal feelings…and strengthening the union of States."[364] While the interactions between Union and Confederate veterans did undoubtedly produce "fraternal feelings," the scars of war in the Shenandoah Valley could never be fully erased and still exist today. From one generation to the next, families pass down stories of hardships confronted during the war as well as artifacts that symbolize the destruction families endured, particularly as a result of Sheridan's operations. For example, a small glass bottle containing wheat burned during Sheridan's Burning complete with a handwritten label—"Burned wheat from the Cline Mill Burned during war of 1864"—has been passed down from one generation to the next in one Augusta County family as "a reminder of Civil War tragedies" experienced during Sheridan's 1864 Shenandoah Campaign.[365]

Although the Civil War has at times left a negative memory of Union operations in the Shenandoah Valley, if one looks closely enough, one can see various attempts, however subtle, to rekindle some of that sentiment of forgiveness evinced between Union and Confederate veterans. During the Civil War centennial, various organizations—including some in the Shenandoah Valley, such as the organizers of the Apple

A bottle of charred wheat passed down from one generation to the next as a reminder of the destruction perpetrated in the Shenandoah Valley during the Burning. *Owen Harner private collection.*

Blossom Festival—looked for ways to turn the centennial into what historian Robert J. Cook labeled "a...pageant." But the Shenandoah County Centennial Commission decided to rekindle an event on a battlefield where Sheridan's Army of the Shenandoah routed General Early's command; thus, it planned another Fisher's Hill reunion.[366] Dormant since 1934, Shenandoah County's Centennial Commission revived the reunion in 1961, not to celebrate the Civil War but rather to commemorate it in homage to the throngs of Union and Confederate veterans who journeyed to that battlefield in the decades after the conflict; voiced their opinions about the war, however divisive they might have been; and engaged in activities intended to promote national healing. The event in 1961 even included a shooting match. While some might construe the shooting match as an attempt at the pageantry so commonplace throughout the centennial, it could also be viewed as a nod of respect to a method Union and Confederate veterans employed to bury old hatreds in the Shenandoah Valley seventy-six years earlier.[367]

The Civil War was in its immediate aftermath, at the time of the Civil War centennial and today, in the words of historian Bruce Catton, "the most significant experience in our national existence."[368] Nothing stirs deeper emotions about our nation's past than the American Civil War because, as Catton aptly noted, the conflict "means so many different things. It emphasizes the point that any great historic truth has many facets."[369] While divisions still exist about issues related to the secession crisis, slavery, the war's origins and emancipation, chasms also remain about how the Civil War was, is and should be remembered."[370]

As the Civil War's sesquicentennial commemoration nears its conclusion, any reasonable historian understands that while much work remains to address those divisions, there is no denying that the foundation for healing the Civil War's wounds was partially laid by interactions between Union and Confederate veterans in the Shenandoah Valley between the 1880s and the early twentieth century. While some today might find fault with the approach Union and Confederate veterans took to national healing in the Shenandoah Valley—what they chose to remember; what they chose, at times, to forget; and what they opted to never let fall into obscurity—it is important to remember, as historian David Blight has so eloquently stated, that in "the wake of the Civil War, there were no 'Truth and Reconciliation' commissions."[371] In short, the veterans' efforts, however flawed they might seem in the hindsight of historical reflection, did what they deemed necessary, in the context of the period in which they lived, to heal the deep wounds of this Republic's greatest tragedy—wounds that, although not as pronounced, still exist today.

The efforts of Union and Confederate veterans to heal the Civil War's wounds in the Shenandoah Valley in the half century after the Civil War's end, regardless of any shortcomings we see today, offer powerful examples of forgiveness, ones that offer us lessons in the present, in the words of Confederate veteran Judge John Paul, to "look calmly at all sides of…questions" and maintain "hope for the future."[372]

APPENDIX A

Note on rosters: for the purpose of honoring the first groups of Union veterans who visited the Shenandoah Valley in 1883 and 1885 and laid the foundation for some degree of postwar healing, the rosters of both excursions are included.

ROSTER OF THE SHERIDAN'S VETERANS' ASSOCIATION

These lists include rank during the time of Sheridan's 1864 Shenandoah Campaign, postwar occupation and residence at the time of the excursion to the Shenandoah Valley. Lists of various committees' membership and civilians who participated in the September 1883 excursion to the Shenandoah Valley are also provided.[373]

Officers of the Sheridan's Veterans' Association

Colonel Carroll D. Wright, president
General Elisha Hunt Rhodes, vice-president
George W. Powers, secretary
Charles Carleton Coffin, treasurer
Reverend Benjamin F. Whittemore, chaplain
Officers of the Excursion
Colonel Carroll D. Wright, commander
Sergeant Francis H. Buffum, excursion manager
Major Ira Berry Jr., chief of staff
Colonel A.C. Wellington, aid
T.C. Bond, aid

Appendix A

Excursion Committee

Colonel Carroll D. Wright
Major F.L. Tolman
Captain C.W. Hodgdon
Captain J.W. Sturtevant

Executive Committee

Colonel Carroll D. Wright
General Stephen Thomas
Captain Allen Baker
Captain W.H. Cunningham
Sergeant F.H. Buffum
Lieutenant G.A. Reed
Chaplain B.F. Whittemore
Captain H.T. Hall
Sergeant J.W. Chapman

Excursion Staff

Captain G.N. Carpenter, adjutant
Reverend B.F Whittemore, chaplain
Captain C.W. Hodgdon, paymaster
Marshall Perkins, surgeon
E.A. Chase, assistant surgeon
Captain W.H. Cunningham, provost marshal
Lieutenant C.G. Howard, quartermaster
Sergeant R. Huntoon, quartermaster sergeant
J.E. Ashley, commissary
C.E. Dudrow, train master

Officers of the Day

Major Ira Berry Jr.
Captain H.T. Hall
Captain C.P. Hall
Colonel A.C. Wellington
Captain W.H. Cunningham

Appendix A

Musicians

C.H. Griffin, bugler
E.J. Hadley, bugler
Albert Cooper, drummer

Excursion Quartette

Miss Anna V. Shaw
Mrs. M.S. Bullock
Lieutenant C.F. Shaw
Major R.S. Ripley, drum major

Guests of the Veterans

William H. Emory, major general in the U.S. Army, commander of the Nineteenth Army Corps, Washington, D.C.
Henry W. Birge, brigadier general, commander of the First Brigade, Second Division, Nineteenth Corps, Boonton, New Jersey

Ladies

Mrs. Thomas C. Bond, Boston, Massachusetts
Miss Annie E.L. Borden, New Bedford, Massachusetts
Mrs. M.S. Bullock, New Bedford, Massachusetts
Mrs. Edwin Burnham, Boston, Massachusetts
Miss L.A. Calef, Washington, Vermont
Mrs. S.R. Coffin, Boston, Massachusetts
Mrs. W. Irving Ellis, Melrose, Massachusetts
Mrs. E.P. George, West Fairlee, Vermont
Miss H.E. Gillette, Cleveland, Ohio
Mrs. W.B. Gove, Washington, D.C.
Mrs. M.E. Hadley, Luverne, Minnesota
Mrs. A.G. Hull, Taintor, Iowa
Mrs. N.R. Lewis, Fall River, Massachusetts
Mrs. A.G. Newcomb, Washington, Vermont
Mrs. C.J. Niles, Thetford, Vermont
Mrs. E.L. Noyes, Boston, Massachusetts
Mrs. Oliver Quimby, Brockton, Massachusetts
Miss Anna V. Shaw, New Bedford, Massachusetts
Mrs. Lizzie S. Stowell, Claremont, New Hampshire
Mrs. Joseph Willis, Canton, Massachusetts

Appendix A

Fourteenth New Hampshire Infantry, Staff

Marshall Perkins, assistant surgeon; physician; Marlow, New Hampshire

Fourteenth New Hampshire Infantry, Company A

Edwin J. Goodnow, private; machinist; Westmoreland, New Hampshire
Charles P. Hall, captain; teacher; Hinsdale, New Hampshire
Asa Knowlton, private; farmer; Dublin, New Hampshire.
Henry Latham, corporal; mechanic; Hinsdale, New Hampshire
David Mason, private; farmer; Dublin, New Hampshire
George O. Wardwell, corporal; house joiner; Keene, New Hampshire

Fourteenth New Hampshire Infantry, Company B

Charles H. Gilbert, musician; dentist; Andover, Massachusetts
Charles R. Gowen, private; hotelkeeper; Springfield, Massachusetts
Charles H. Jennison, sergeant; merchant; Chicago, Illinois
Jonathan Turner, corporal; furniture manufacturer; Ayer, Massachusetts

Fourteenth New Hampshire Infantry, Company D

Albert Gove, private; farmer; Seabrook, New Hampshire
D. Hadley Elbridge, lieutenant; lawyer; Luverne, Minnesota
C.W. Hodgon, captain; dentist; 169 Court Street, Boston, Massachusetts

Fourteenth New Hampshire Infantry, Company I

Charles B. Comings, sergeant; furniture; Lebanon, New Hampshire
Harlan P. Hunter, private; mechanic; Claremont, New Hampshire
Ransom Huntoon, sergeant; cloth folder; Newport, New Hampshire
Henry C. Mase, private; teamster; Claremont, New Hampshire
John Santry, private; saloonkeeper; Lynn, Massachusetts
George H. Stowell Jr., sergeant; manufacturer; Claremont, New Hampshire

Fourteenth New Hampshire Infantry, Company C

Ira Berry Jr., brevet major; merchant; Portland, Maine
Carroll L. Coombs, private; mechanic; West Dummerston, Vermont
Carroll D. Wright, colonel; chief of Massachusetts Bureau of Statistics;
Boston, Massachusetts

Appendix A

Fourteenth New Hampshire Infantry, Company F

Henry E. Baldwin, corporal; sawyer; Winchester, New Hampshire
James H. Bolton, private; farmer; Ashuelot, New Hampshire
Francis H. Buffum, color sergeant; journalist, *Herald* office; Boston, Massachusetts
George A. Day, bandleader; carpenter; Hinsdale, New Hampshire
Chauncey S. Farr, private; machinist; Hinsdale, New Hampshire
Charles G. Howard, lieutenant; gardener; Springfield, Massachusetts
Daniel H. Thompson, corporal; farmer; Winchester, New Hampshire

Fourteenth New Hampshire Infantry, Company G

Albert Cooper, musician; expressman; Boston, Massachusetts
Herbert C. Hatch, private; farmer; Bellow Falls, Vermont
Edward B. Howard, lieutenant; pork packer; New York
Marion D. Learned, corporal; fruit grower; South Vineland, New Jersey
N.W. Mower, musician; railroad agent; East Jaffrey, New Hampshire
S. Albert Pierce, corporal; locomotive machinist; Fitchburg, Massachusetts
Joel H. Poole, private; summer hotel; Jaffrey, New Hampshire
James W. Russell, lieutenant; merchant; Keene, New Hampshire
John W. Sturtevant, captain; books and stationery; Keene, New Hampshire
Flavel L. Tolman, major; furniture manufacturer, Leominster, Massachusetts
Henry A. Turner, sergeant; livery keeper; Gardner, Massachusetts

Thirty-fourth Massachusetts Infantry

Henry Bemis, corporal; boot cutter; Spencer, Massachusetts
George Bliss, private; provision dealer; West Warren, Massachusetts
Ephraim C. Carey, private; farmer; Warren, Massachusetts
William H.H. Cheney, musician; farmer; Southbridge, Massachusetts
George Congdon, sergeant; overseer; Fall River, Massachusetts
George W. Corey, corporal; assistant postmaster; Southbridge, Massachusetts
Charles H. Giffin, musician; mail carrier; Brookfield, Massachusetts
Lucian W. Gilbert, private; machinist; Warren, Massachusetts
Henry T. Hall, captain; treasurer, manufacturing company; 179 Devonshire
    Street, Boston, Massachusetts
Harlan P. Houghton, lieutenant; carpenter; Providence, Rhode Island
Joseph H. Lombard, private; foreman, boot factory; North Brookfield,
    Massachusetts
Andrew H. Morse, private; farmer; Southbridge, Massachusetts
James A. Needham, corporal; overseer; Clinton, Massachusetts
Melville E. Walker, captain; manufacturer; Providence, Rhode Island

Robert W. Walker, lieutenant; shirt cutter; Boston, Massachusetts
Austin F. Wilson, private; conductor, OCRR; Boston, Massachusetts

Thirty-eighth Massachusetts Infantry

Arthur S. Byrnes, first sergeant; Plymouth, Massachusetts
James W. Chapman, first sergeant; commissioner of deeds; Boston, Massachusetts
John P. DeLacy, private; soldier's messenger corps; Boston, Massachusetts
Frank M. Flynn, private; dyer; Lynn, Massachusetts
Charles C. Howland, captain; grocer; Boston, Massachusetts
Alphonso M. Lunt, sergeant; railway postal clerk; East Cambridge, Massachusetts
George W. Powers, corporal; proofreader; Boston, Massachusetts
Thomas R. Rodman, captain; accountant; New Bedford, Massachusetts
Charles F. Shaw, lieutenant; wholesale grocer; New Bedford, Massachusetts
William A. Turnbull, lieutenant; salesman; 110 North Street, Boston, Massachusetts
Austin C. Wellington, acting adjutant; now colonel, First Regiment MVM; coal dealer; Boston, Massachusetts
William H. Whitney, captain; civil engineer and surveyor; Boston, Massachusetts

Third Massachusetts Cavalry

George Armstrong, corporal; cabinetmaker; Everett, Massachusetts
William H. Cunningham, lieutenant; engine fire department, city hall; Boston, Massachusetts
Charles T. Emery, sergeant; clerk; Boston, Massachusetts
Milan H. Harris, sergeant; watchman; Leominster, Massachusetts
James W. Hervey, captain; banker; New Bedford, Massachusetts
Samuel W. Lewis, lieutenant; news dealer; Danvers, Massachusetts
Edward L. Noyes, captain; provision dealer; 3 Wellington Street, Boston, Massachusetts
Henry D. Pope, lieutenant, also assistant inspector general, Third Brigade, Second Division, Nineteenth Corps; paper dealer; 91 Federal Street, Boston, Massachusetts
J. Cushing Thomas, corporal; carriage builder; Boston, Massachusetts

Twenty-sixth Massachusetts Infantry

Frank S. Berry, private; clerk; Lowell, Massachusetts
Alonzo Bowman, private; chief of police; Brookline, Massachusetts
James Brady Jr., captain; collector of customs; Fall River, Massachusetts

Delette H. Hall, commissary sergeant; woodenware manufacturer; West Acton, Massachusetts

L. Hosley, private; bookbinder; Fitchburg, Massachusetts

George A. Reed, lieutenant; railroad conductor; Saxonville, Massachusetts

Frank H. Stevens, sergeant; farmer; West Acton, Massachusetts

Stephen W. Wheeler, corporal; farmer; New Ipswich, New Hampshire

Eleventh Vermont Infantry

Edwin Burnham, corporal; clerk, B&ARR; Boston, Massachusetts

E.R. Campbell, private, also First Artillery; clerk; Brandon, Vermont

George N. Carpenter, captain, also captain CSUS Volunteers; insurance; Boston, Massachusetts

W.H. Gibson, private, also First Artillery; shoemaker; Cambridge, New York

R.E. Hathorn, private, also First Artillery; harness dealer; Ludlow, Vermont

Lucien A. Lamson, musician; druggist; Hinsdale, New Hampshire

Albert Patch, lieutenant; clerk; 160 Cambridge Street, Boston, Massachusetts

Eighth Vermont Infantry

H.H. Gillett, surgeon; physician and farmer; Post Mills, Vermont

W.H. Gilmore, quartermaster sergeant; farmer; Fairlee, Vermont

Stephen Thomas, colonel; famer; Montpelier, Vermont

James Welch, lieutenant; famer; Randolph, Vermont

First Rhode Island Cavalry

Allen Baker Jr., captain, escort headquarters cavalry corps; merchant; Providence, Rhode Island

William Gardner, sergeant; police; Providence, Rhode Island

Thomas W. Manchester, captain; jeweler; Providence, Rhode Island

Thirteenth Massachusetts Infantry

John F. Childs, private; shoemaker; Natick, Massachusetts

David F. Fiske, corporal; clerk; Natick, Massachusetts

Joseph H. Twichell, private; government clerk; Washington, D.C.

Appendix A

Maine, Miscellaneous Units

Isaac H. Danforth, First Battery; granite worker; Brunswick, Maine

Oliver B. Quimby, private, First Battery; shoe manufacturer; Brockton, Massachusetts

S.L. Johnson, sergeant, Fifth Infantry; clerk; Chelsea, Massachusetts

Edward W. Thompson, lieutenant, Twelfth Infantry; solicitor of patents; Lowell, Massachusetts

Thomas W. Porter, colonel, Fourteenth Infantry; attorney at law; 33 School Street, Boston, Massachusetts

James E. Alexander, Fifteenth Infantry; provision dealer; Brunswick, Maine

E.A. Chase, private, Twenty-ninth Infantry; physician; Brockton, Massachusetts

Sewall D. Goodwin, seaman, USS *Monitor Nahant*; tinsmith; Wells, Maine

New Hampshire, Miscellaneous Units

William W. Fish, private, Eleventh Infantry; clerk; West Somerville, Massachusetts

Edgar J. Hadley, bugler, First Cavalry; machinist; Athol, Massachusetts

Albert H. Taft, corporal, Ninth Infantry; physician; Winchester, New Hampshire

Lorenzo M. Upham, private, Ninth Infantry; wool sorter; Hinsdale, New Hampshire

Vermont, Miscellaneous Units

Hiram P. Bixby, private, Second Infantry; farmer; Ludlow, Vermont

Thomas C. Bond, private, Tenth Infantry; cutter; Boston, Massachusetts

Austin W. Fuller, lieutenant, Tenth Infantry; furniture dealer; St. Albans, Vermont

Massachusetts, Miscellaneous Units

Henry E. Alvord, captain, Second Cavalry; provost marshal, cavalry reserve brigade; farmer and teacher, Mountainville, New York

Lucius Richmond, captain, Fourth Cavalry; paints and oils; Brockton, Massachusetts

William C. Griffin, sergeant, Sixteenth Infantry; leather cutter; North Brookfield, Massachusetts

Walter Winward, private, Sixteenth Infantry; clerk; Somerville, Massachusetts

Royal S. Ripley, drum major, Thirtieth Infantry; North Chelmsford, Massachusetts

Benjamin F. Whittemore, chaplain, Thirtieth Infantry; ex-congressman; publisher; 32 Hawley Street, Boston, Massachusetts

William H. Abbott, sergeant, Thirty-seventh Infantry; hotelkeeper; Neponset, Massachusetts

William A. Ely, private, Thirty-seventh Infantry; express agent; Johnstown, New York

Nathan Reed, sergeant, Thirty-ninth Infantry; shoemaker; Natick, Massachusetts

John E. Ashley, private, Forty-fifth Infantry; salesman; Somerville, Massachusetts

E.T. Morse, private, Forty-fifth Infantry; agent, Adams Express Company; Southbridge, Massachusetts

Samuel Currier, sergeant, Fifty-ninth Infantry; leather sorter; Natick, Massachusetts

Rhode Island, Miscellaneous Units

Elisha H. Rhodes, colonel, Second Infantry; U.S. collector internal revenue; commander of the Rhode Island militia; Providence, Rhode Island

Joshua M. Addeman, captain, Fourteenth Heavy Artillery; secretary of state; Providence, Rhode Island

Charles D. Worthington, sergeant, Battery B; engineer; Spencer, Massachusetts

Connecticut, Miscellaneous Units

Charles H. Briggs, captain, First Cavalry; clerk; Harpers Ferry, West Virginia

J.D. Willis, sergeant, First Cavalry; Willimantic, Connecticut

Lawrence O'Brien, captain, Ninth Infantry; builder; New Haven, Connecticut

Leonard A. Dickinson, captain, Twelfth Infantry; assistant adjutant general, Second Brigade, First Division, Nineteenth Corps; postmaster; Hartford, Connecticut

James E. Smith, adjutant and captain, Twelfth Infantry; bookkeeper; Hartford, Connecticut

New York, Miscellaneous Units

W.G. Martens, private, 116th Infantry; jeweler; Rochester, New York

Charles G. Otis, colonel, Twenty-first Cavalry, Second Division, Cavalry Corps; elevator manufacturer; 92 Liberty Street, New York

Charles H. Yost, sergeant, 140th Infantry; auctioneer; Rochester, New York

George W. Graham, lieutenant, 144th Infantry; lawyer; Harpers Ferry, West Virginia

Pennsylvania, Miscellaneous Units

Charles E. Dudrow, chief saddler, Fourteenth Cavalry; traveling passenger agent, Baltimore & Ohio Railroad; Harpers Ferry, West Virginia

Appendix A

Maryland, Miscellaneous Units

George H. Reynolds, private, First Infantry; calker; Harpers Ferry, West Virginia

Ohio, Miscellaneous Units

William H. Abbott, corporal, Twenty-ninth Infantry; soap manufacturer; Holkoke, Massachusetts

West Virginia, Miscellaneous Units

J.H. Bristor, major, Twelfth Infantry; real estate; Martinsburg, West Virginia
Albert G. Hull, sergeant, Twelfth Infantry; farmer; Taintor, Iowa

Regular Army

L.F. Upright, bugler, Battery L, First Artillery; butcher; Harpers Ferry, West Virginia

Sons of Veterans

Charles Huntoon, Newport, New Hampshire
George B. King, Boston, Massachusetts
Ernie, Latham, Hinsdale, New Hampshire
Harry H. Pope, Boston, Massachusetts

Civilians

W.O. Amidon, Hinsdale, New Hampshire
W.S. Briggs, Keene, New Hampshire
C.M. Bromwich, South Boston, Massachusetts
M.S. Cahill, Boston, Massachusetts
Ira C. Calef, Washington, Vermont
Charles Carleton Coffin, Boston, Massachusetts
Frederic O. Clark, South, Boston, Massachusetts
William R. Clough, Marlow, New Hampshire
H. Cowles, MD, Saxonville, Massachusetts
Frank S. Currier, Natick, Massachusetts
C.N. Farnsworth, North Leominster, Massachusetts
Albert F. Fish, Cambridge, Massachusetts
D.W. Fletcher, Hinsdale, New Hampshire
C.A. Fretts, Leominster, Massachusetts

Appendix A

Elbridge B. Gee, Marlow, New Hampshire
E.P. George, West Fairlee, Vermont
W.B. Gove, Washington, D.C.
George A. Hall, Roxbury, New Hampshire
C.D. Holt, West Gardner, Massachusetts
Martin S. Leach, Hinsdale, Massachusetts
Fred S. Leonard, Hinsdale, New Hampshire
N.R. Lewis, Fall River, Massachusetts
Honorable A.H. Littlefield, Pawtucket, Rhode Island
A. Magoon, Danvers, Massachusetts
J. Carlton Nichols, South Boston, Massachusetts
Caleb H. Packard, Brockton, Massachusetts
W.E. Phelps, North Leominster, Massachusetts
Cyrus Piper, Keene, New Hampshire
Thomas Raynor, South Boston, Massachusetts
Artemus Richard, South Boston, Massachusetts
C.C. Riley, Washington, D.C.
A.B. Skinner, Keene, New Hampshire
F.C. Stearns, Saxonville, Massachusetts
Edwin D. Stickney, Boston, Massachusetts
E.C. Stone, Lynn, Massachusetts
J.A. Stowell, Leominster, Massachusetts
Washington Tufts, Brookfield, Massachusetts
J. Ashley Turner, Willimantic, Massachusetts
A.V. Walker, North Leominster, Massachusetts
Nathan M. Worden, Hinsdale, Massachusetts

APPENDIX B

Roster of the Sheridan's Veterans' Association

These lists include members of various rifle teams, Confederate veterans of the Gray rifle team and civilians who participated in the September 1885 excursion to the Shenandoah Valley.[374]

Officers of the Sheridan's Veterans' Association

Colonel Carroll D. Wright, president
General Elisha H. Rhodes, vice-president
Corporal George W. Powers, secretary
Honorable Charles Carleton Coffin, treasurer
Honorable Benjamin F. Whittemore, chaplain
Marshall Perkins, surgeon
E.A. Chase, assistant surgeon

Staff

General L.A. Dickinson, chief of staff and adjutant
Colonel George N. Carpenter, Major E.L. Noyes, aides

Excursion Manager

Captain Francis H. Buffum

APPENDIX B

Excursion Staff

Captain C.W. Hodgdon, paymaster
Sergeant R. Huntoon, quartermaster
Corporal George W. Powers, commissary
Sergeant U.B. Fosgate, quartermaster sergeant
Charles E. Dudrow, train master
Captain E.D. Hadley, Dr. E.D. Stickney, aides
Colonel Austin C. Wellington, chief of rifle practice
Captain L. O'Brien, Colonel W.H. Gilmore, aides

Officers of the Day

Wednesday: Captain C.C. Howland
Thursday: Captain J.E. Smith
Friday: Captain S.E. Howard
Saturday: Captain W.H. Cunningham
Sunday: none listed
Monday: Captain J.W. Hervey
Alonzo Bowman, chief of camp police
J.A. French, excursion photographer
Charles W. Gould, excursion stenographer

Rifle Teams

THE BLUE TEAM FOR THE BLUE-GRAY MATCH
Captain Francis H. Buffum, Fourteenth New Hampshire Infantry (team captain)
Lieutenant F.C. Forbes, Eighth Vermont Infantry
Sergeant M.A. Harris, Third Massachusetts Cavalry
Captain C.W. Hodgdon, Fourteenth New Hampshire Infantry
Lieutenant G.A. Reed, Twenty-sixth Massachusetts Infantry
Lieutenant James Welch, Eighth Vermont Infantry
Colonel Austin C. Wellington, Thirty-eighth Massachusetts Infantry

THE GRAY TEAM FOR THE BLUE-GRAY MATCH
Captain J.A. Nulton, Second Virginia Infantry, Stonewall Brigade (team captain)
F. Blankner, First Virginia Infantry, Evans Brigade
William Calvert, Fifth Virginia Infantry, Stonewall Brigade
Hodson, Virginia Cavalry
John McCoy, Thirty-third Virginia Infantry, Stonewall Brigade
Striker, Virginia Cavalry
R.E. Trenary, Fifth Virginia Infantry, Stonewall Brigade

APPENDIX B

Union Regimental Rifle Teams That Competed Against Each Other in a Special Competition at Winchester

THIRD MASSACHUSETTS CAVALRY RIFLE TEAM
Major. E.L. Noyes (team captain)
Captain. W.H. Cunningham, Company G
Lieutenant N.S. Dixey, Company D
Captain J.W. Hervey, Company A
Sergeant M.A. Harris, Company M

EIGHTH VERMONT INFANTRY RIFLE TEAM
Captain S.E. Howard (team captain)
Lieutenant James Welch
Captain Moses McFarland
Sergeant A.H. Ward
F.C. Forbes

FOURTEENTH NEW HAMPSHIRE RIFLE TEAM
Captain F.H. Buffum, Company F (captain)
Sergeant U.B. Fosgate, Company F
Captain C.W. Hodgon, Company D
William H. Hodgon, Company D
Corporal D.H. Tompkins, Company F

TWENTY-SIXTH MASSACHUSETTS RIFLE TEAM
Captain James Brady Jr. (captain)
Alonzo Bowman
Lieutenant G.A. Reed
Sergeant D.H. Hall
E.D. Lothrop

THIRTY-EIGHTH MASSACHUSETTS RIFLE TEAM
Colonel A.C. Wellington (captain)
Captain C.C. Howland
C.S. Peterson
Corporal G.W. Powers
Lieutenant C.F. Shaw

Ladies

Mrs. William Billings, Canton, Massachusetts
Miss Kitty Blake, New Haven Connecticut

Appendix B

Mrs. T.C. Bond, Boston, Massachusetts
Miss A.E.L. Borden, New Bedford, Massachusetts
Mrs. M.S. Cahill, Boston, Massachusetts
Mrs. L.H. Clough, Marlow, New Hampshire
Mrs. W.H. Cunningham, Boston, Massachusetts
Mrs. C.P. Davis, Newburyport, Massachusetts
Mrs. C.W. Day, South Royalston, Massachusetts
Miss Ella C. Deane, Canton, Massachusetts
Mrs. T.B. Draper, Canton, Massachusetts
Mrs. L.M. Drury, Worcester, Massachusetts
Mrs. George Fairbanks, Natick, Massachusetts
Mrs. David Fisk, Natick, Massachusetts
Mrs. E.S. Foster, New Haven, Connecticut
Mrs. L.P. Gleason, Montpelier, Vermont
Mrs. M.E. Hadley, Luverne, Minnesota
Mrs. G.G. Hall, Boston, Massachusetts
Miss K.H. Hannan, Lynn, Massachusetts
Miss C.I. Harris, Leominster, Massachusetts
Mrs. Joseph Harrison, Fall River, Massachusetts
Mrs. J.W. Hervey, New Bedford, Massachusetts
Mrs. Monroe Holcomb, New Bedford, Massachusetts
Mrs. Grenville Hovey, Boston, Massachusetts
Mrs. H.W. Howe, Waltham, Massachusetts
Mrs. C.C. Howland, Boston, Massachusetts
Mrs. Frank Kirk, New Bedford, Massachusetts
Miss F.K. Leavitt, Canton, Massachusetts
Mrs. N.R. Lewis, Fall River, Massachusetts
Miss A.K. Mead, Randolph, Vermont
Mrs. J.B. Mead, Randolph, Vermont
Miss N.O. Mead, Randolph, Vermont
Mrs. N.W. Mower, East Jaffrey, New Hampshire
Mrs. A.T. Newcomb, Montpelier, Vermont
Mrs. E.L. Noyes, Boston, Massachusetts
Mrs. E.J. Ormsbee, Brandon, Vermont
Miss L.C. Peterson, Marshfield, Massachusetts
Mrs. D.S. Ray, East Providence, Rhode Island
Mrs. E.H. Rhodes, Providence, Rhode Island
Miss Rhodes, Providence, Rhode Island
Mrs. R.S. Ripley, North Chelmsford, Massachusetts
Miss A.V. Shaw, New Bedford, Massachusetts
Mrs. F.E. Smith, Montpelier, Vermont
Mrs. J.E. Smith, Hartford, Connecticut

Appendix B

Mrs. L.M. Upham, Hinsdale, New Hampshire
Mrs. Grace Whittemore, Montvale, Massachusetts
Mrs. J.W. Willis, Canton, Massachusetts

The following portion of the roster lists members of the SVA in attendance by regimental affiliation and includes, where applicable, occupations and places of residence at the time of their excursion to the Shenandoah Valley in 1885.

Eighth Vermont Infantry

G.N. Carpenter, colonel, insurance, 31 Milk Street, Boston, Massachusetts
F.C. Forbes, lieutenant, South Burlington, Vermont
H.H. Gilette, surgeon, physician and farmer; Post Mills, Vermont
W.H. Gilmore, quartermaster sergeant, colonel, farmer, Bradford, Vermont
S.E. Howard, captain, corporation treasurer, West Newton, Massachusetts
J.B. Mead, colonel, Randolph, Vermont
Moses McFarland, captain, Waterville, Vermont
E.J. Ormsbee, captain, lieutenant governor, Brandon, Vermont
F.E. Smith, captain, Montpelier, Vermont
Stephen Thomas, brigadier general, brevet major general, farmer, Montpelier, Vermont
A.H. Ward, sergeant, Montague, Massachusetts
James Welch, lieutenant, farmer, Randolph, Vermont

Fourteenth New Hampshire Infantry

I.E. Brown, private, shoemaker, Kensington, New Hampshire
F.H. Buffum, color sergeant; captain; editorial staff, *Herald*; Boston, Massachusetts
U.B. Fosgate, sergeant, mechanic, Winchester, New Hampshire
C.R. Gowen, private, hotel proprietor, Franklin, Massachusetts
E.D. Hadley, captain, banker, Luverne, Massachusetts
C.W. Hodgdon, captain; dentist; 169 Court Street, Boston, Massachusetts
W.H. Hodgdon, musician, farmer, Kensington, New Hampshire
H.P. Hunter, sergeant, mechanic, Brattleboro, Vermont
Ransom Huntoon, sergeant, cloth folder, Newport, New Hampshire
N.W. Mower, musician, railroad agent, East Jaffrey, New Hampshire
D.H. Thompson, corporal, farmer, Winchester, New Hampshire
C.D. Wright, colonel; chief, Massachusetts Bureau of Statistics of Labor; chief, National Bureau Statistics of Labor; Boston, Massachusetts

Appendix B

Third Massachusetts Cavalry

W.H. Cunningham, captain, mill inspector, Boston, Massachusetts
N.S. Dickey, lieutenant, Boston, Massachusetts
M.A. Harris, sergeant, watchman, Leominster, Massachusetts
J.W. Hervey, captain, banker, New Bedford, Massachusetts
Monroe Holcomb, corporal, New Bedford, Massachusetts
H.K. Lyman, Boston, Massachusetts
E.L. Noyes, captain, provision dealer, 3 Wellington Street, Boston, Massachusetts
A.H. Shattuck, Washington, D.C.

Twenty-sixth Massachusetts Infantry

Alonzo Bowman, private, chief of police, Brookline, Massachusetts
James Brady Jr., captain, collector of customs, Fall River, Massachusetts
L.V. Clough, private, South Acton, Massachusetts
Joseph Harrison, sergeant, Fall River, Massachusetts
E.D. Lathrop, Milford, Massachusetts
G.A. Reed, lieutenant, railroad conductor, Saxonville, Massachusetts

Thirty-eighth Massachusetts Infantry

William Friend, private, canvasser, Boston, Massachusetts
C.C. Howland, captain, grocer, Boston, Massachusetts
C.S. Peterson, private, Marshfield, Massachusetts
G.W. Powers, corporal, proofreader, Boston, Massachusetts
C.F. Shaw, lieutenant, wholesale grocer, New Bedford, Massachusetts
A.C. Wellington, acting adjutant, now colonel First Regiment, MVM; Austin
    C. Wellington Coal Company; 17 Congress Street, Boston, Massachusetts.

First Rhode Island Cavalry

Lyman Aylesworth, East Greenwich, Rhode Island
D.S. Ray, quartermaster sergeant, hardware dealer, East Providence, Rhode Island
R.E. Schouler, sergeant, manufacturer, Blackington, Massachusetts

Thirtieth Massachusetts Infantry

H.W. Howe, captain, lumber dealer, Waltham, Massachusetts
R.S. Ripley, drum major, salesman, North Chelmsford, Massachusetts
B.F. Whittemore, chaplain; ex-congressman; publisher; 32 Hawley Street,
    Boston, Massachusetts

Appendix B

First, Tenth, Twenty-ninth Maine Infantry

R.W. Randall, private, Auburn, Maine

Members from Various New Hampshire Units

Reverend C.H. Kimball, captain, Berdan Sharpshooters; Baptist ministry; Manchester, New Hampshire

Lorenzo M. Upham, private, Ninth Infantry; wool sorter; Hinsdale, New Hampshire

Members from Various Vermont Units

T.C. Bond, private, Tenth Infantry; cutter; Boston, Massachusetts

W.W. Grout, lieutenant colonel, Fifteenth Infantry; member of Congress; Barton, Vermont

L.B. Newcomb, Montpelier, Vermont

Albert Patch, Eleventh Infantry, clerk, Boston, Massachusetts

L.K. Stiles, First Cavalry, Keene, New Hampshire

Frank Stockwell, captain, Brattleboro, Vermont

Members from Various Massachusetts Units

George Bliss, private, Thirty-fourth Infantry; provision dealer; West Warren, Massachusetts

J.P. Crane, captain, Twenty-second Infantry; Woburn, Massachusetts

C.E. Davis, Fifth Infantry, clerk, Somerville, Massachusetts

J.M. Day, Seventh Infantry, policeman, Boston, Massachusetts

D.H. Fisk, Thirty-ninth Infantry, clerk, Natick, Massachusetts

William Gibbs, colonel, First Cavalry; Waltham, Massachusetts

J.W. Haines, corporal, Seventeenth Infantry; Danver, Massachusetts

W.H. Nichols, corporal, Company A, Seventh Squadron, Rhode Island Cavalry; also private, Company I, Sixth Infantry; leather dealer; Salem, Massachusetts

G.H. Patch, private, Company I, Nineteenth Infantry; journalist, South Framingham, Massachusetts

T.P. Smith, corporal, Forty-fifth Infantry; publisher; Waltham, Massachusetts

Nathan Warren, corporal, Forty-fifth Infantry; insurance; Waltham, Massachusetts

J.E. Wright, sergeant, Thirty-fourth Infantry; Montpelier, Vermont

APPENDIX B

Members from Various Rhode Island Units

F.W. Graves, MD, Seventh Squadron, Rhode Island Cavalry; Woburn, Massachusetts

E.H. Rhodes, colonel, Second Infantry; commander of the Rhode Island Militia; Providence, Rhode Island

Members from Various Connecticut Units

E.K. Bradley, private, Company K, First Cavalry; Meriden, Connecticut

N.A. Bosworth, sergeant, First Cavalry; steamfitter; Hartford, Connecticut

L.A. Dickinson, captain, Twelfth Infantry; assistant adjutant general, Second Brigade, First Division, Nineteenth Corps; adjutant general of Connecticut; insurance; Hartford, Connecticut

Lawrence O'Brien, captain, Ninth Infantry; builder; New Haven, Connecticut

J.E. Smith, adjutant and captain, Twelfth Infantry; bookkeeper; Hartford, Connecticut

J.O. Stoughton, Second Artillery, Ferryville, Connecticut

Henry Upson, chaplain, Thirteenth Infantry; New Preston, Connecticut

Members from Various New York Units

C.B. Everts, First Cavalry, Windsor, Vermont

R.H. Jackson, Hawkins' Zouaves, Ninth Infantry; Providence, Rhode Island

Alfred Neafie, colonel, 156th Infantry, brevet brigadier general, U.S. Volunteers; insurance and real estate; Goshen, New York

Members from Various Pennsylvania Units

C.E. Dudrow, chief saddler, Fourteenth Cavalry; traveling passenger agent Baltimore & Ohio Railroad; Harpers Ferry, West Virginia

Civilians

W.E. Adams, Montpelier, Vermont

Shiro Akabane, Washington, D.C.

E.C. Bliss, West Warren, Massachusetts

C.H. Boody, Cochituate, Massachusetts

H.W. Butler, Cochituate, Massachusetts

W.R. Clough, Marlow, New Hampshire

Honorable C.C. Coffin, Boston, Massachusetts

Edward Conant, Randolph, Vermont
George Cushman, Canton, Massachusetts
C.P. Davis, Newburyport, Massachusetts
C.W. Day, South Royalston, Massachusetts
L.M. Drury, Worcester, Massachusetts
A.G. Eaton, Montpelier, Vermont
F.R. Ellis, Winchester, New Hampshire
G.C. Fairbanks, Natick, Massachusetts
J.A. French, Keene, New Hampshire
L.P. Gleason, Montpelier, Vermont
C.W. Gould, Boston, Massachusetts
Jerome Hastings, Natick, Massachusetts
Hovey Grenville, Boston, Massachusetts
S.J. Hoxie, Providence, Rhode Island
Professor R.W. Hulburd, Hyde Park, Vermont
Daniel Johnson
N.R. Lewis, Fall River, Massachusetts
E.C. Masten, Boston, Massachusetts
H.M. McFarland, Hyde Park, Vermont
C.C. Meade, Randolph, Vermont
G.W. Melony, Willimantic, Connecticut
J.A. Moulton, Lexington, Massachusetts
Dr. Luther Newcomb, Montpelier, Vermont
S. Newcomb, Montpelier, Vermont
J.B. Niver, Jamaica Plain, Massachusetts
C.H. Packard, Campello, Massachusetts
W.C. Peck, Montpelier, Vermont
W.P. Perry, Danvers, Massachusetts
W.H. Philbrick, Keene, New Hampshire
M.H. Ray, East Providence, Rhode Island
W.G. Reed, Boston, Massachusetts
O.A. Sessions, Willimantic, Connecticut
G.C. Shedd, Keene, New Hampshire
F.P. Simonds, Natick, Massachusetts
Thomas Smith, Waltham, Massachusetts
E.C. Stevens, West Acton, Massachusetts
J.V. Stevens, Waterville, Connecticut
Dr. E.D. Stickney, Boston, Massachusetts
H.N. Taplin, Montpelier, Vermont
H.W. Taylor, Winchester, New Hampshire
C.N. Thomas, Boston, Massachusetts

Appendix B

H.F. Warren, Waltham, Massachusetts
Willard Warren, Waltham, Massachusetts
B.T. Wells, Boston, Massachusetts
B.T. Wells Jr., Boston, Massachusetts

NOTES

PREFACE

1. Walker Percy, "The American War," in Samway, *Walker Percy*, 71–73.
2. For a historiographical survey of literature on Civil War memory, see Caroline E. Janney, "Memory," in Sheehan-Dean, *Companion*, 2:1,139–54.
3. Shenandoah Valley Battlefields Foundation, *Shenandoah Valley Battlefields*, i.

INTRODUCTION

4. Davis, *Shenandoah*, 273.
5. For an example of how the financial hardships created stresses that, at least in the Shenandoah Valley, pushed some to an early grave, see Noyalas, *Stonewall Jackson's 1862 Valley Campaign*, 45.
6. Davis, *Shenandoah*, 3–4.
7. For further discussion on what Union veterans believed about the Civil War and their affinity for the Union after the conflict, see Gallagher, *Union War*, 151–62.
8. For a discussion of how and why the Civil War still stirs tremendous emotion today, see Goldfield, *Still Fighting the Civil War*.
9. In his recent and thought-provoking book, M. Keith Harris concluded: "Rarely did veterans meet face to face with their former enemies when revisiting wartime memories." If Harris's observation is, in fact, correct, then the Shenandoah Valley offers a remarkable exception, as Union veterans from their first sojourn to the Shenandoah Valley in 1883 through their visits in the early 1900s constantly interacted with Confederate veterans as they confronted their "wartime memories." See Harris, *Across the Bloody Chasm*, 9.
10. Davis, *Shenandoah*, 316.

CHAPTER 1

11. Trowbridge, *South,* 69.

12. Ibid.

13. *New York Herald*, May 22, 1867.

14. Robert T. Barton Memoirs, quoted in Colt, *Defend the Valley*, 377.

15. Opie, *A Rebel*, 254.

16. The statistics on the Shenandoah Valley's outputs in 1860 is based on the statistical tables in Mahon, *Shenandoah Valley*, 133.

17. *Valley Virginian*, August 1, 1866.

18. *New York Herald*, May 22, 1867.

19. Ibid.

20. Ibid.

21. Ibid.

22. Neff, *Honoring the Civil War Dead*, 146.

23. For further discussion on this, see *History of the Confederated Memorial Associations of the South*, 315–16; *History of the Ladies' Confederate Memorial Association*, 3–4; Janney, *Burying the Dead*, 39.

24. *Winchester News*, June 8, 1866. For additional discussion on the prohibitive measures enacted by the Federal government after the war regarding Confederate symbols, see Blair, *Contesting the Memory*, 52–61.

25. *Winchester News*, June 8, 1866.

26. J. Miller Long, "First Confederate Memorial, June 6, 1866," Turner Ashby Camp Papers. Items from this repository hereafter cited as HL.

27. Ibid.

28. Avirett, *Memoirs of General Turner Ashby*, 243; Duncan, *Beleaguered Winchester*, 261; Noyalas, *Plagued by War*, 169.

29. *Staunton Spectator*, August 29, 1865.

30. *Evening Star*, February 15, 1913.

31. King and Derby, *Camp-Fire Sketches*, 513.

32. *Valley Virginian*, October 27, 1870.

33. For a brief discussion of the evolution of total war in the Shenandoah Valley from Hunter to Sheridan, see Mountcastle, *Punitive War*, 121–28. For a scholarly assessment of the impact of Sheridan's 1864 Shenandoah Campaign on the Shenandoah Valley's landscape, see Brady, *War Upon the Land*, 72–92. For the best overall treatment of the Burning and its impact on the Shenandoah Valley, see Heatwole, *Burning.*

34. These figures are derived from General Philip H. Sheridan's report of property destroyed or captured during the 1864 Shenandoah Campaign. See Mahon, *Shenandoah Valley*, 135.

35. Phillips, *Lower Shenandoah Valley*, 167.

36. Casler, *Four Years*, 241.

37. Douglas, *I Rode with Stonewall*, 315.

38. Gallagher and Nolan, *Myth of the Lost Cause*, 13.

39. Pollard, *Southern History of the War*, 109.

40. Horton, *Youth's History*, ii.

41. Ibid., 338–39.

42. It is important to note that while many of the Shenandoah Valley's inhabitants viewed Sheridan's campaign of destruction as reprehensible, some of the men who carried out the directive to destroy the Shenandoah Valley also found it too much to take. For example, Union colonel James H. Kidd, a cavalry officer who served under General George Armstrong Custer's command in the Shenandoah Valley, carried out the orders given to him to destroy mills, barns and crops but could not stand the work he was ordered to perform. Kidd wrote: "What I saw there is burned in my memory. Women with children in their arms, stood in the street and gazed frantically upon the threatened ruin of their homes, while the tears rained down their cheeks. The anguish pictured in their faces would have melted any heart not seared by the horrors and 'necessities' of war. It was too much for me and at the first moment that duty would permit I hurried from the scene." For further discussion, see Starr, *Union Cavalry*, 302–3.

43. Opie, *Rebel Cavalryman*, 254–55.

44. Casler, *Four Years*, 241.

45. Shenandoah Valley Battlefields Foundation, *Shenandoah Valley Battlefields National Historic District*, i.

46. Davidson, *Civil War Letters*, 24–25.

47. Taylor, *With Sheridan Up the Shenandoah Valley*, 116, 118.

48. Creed Thomas Davis diary, September 3, 1864, quoted in Nelson, *Ruin Nation*, 135. The original diary is in the collections of the Virginia Historical Society, Richmond, VA.

49. Wenger and Rodes, *Unionists and the Civil War Experience*, 354.

50. Ibid., 584.

51. Pritchard Claim, Southern Claims Commission Reports, M1407, Nos. 4051–5053.

52. *Winchester Journal*, March 16, 1866.

53. Ibid., April 12, 1866.

54. Ibid., May 3, 1867.

55. Sheridan, *Personal Memoirs*, 1:500.

56. President Abraham Lincoln to General Ulysses S. Grant, September 12, 1864, quoted in Basler, *Collected Works*, 548.

57. In some previous works, Laws has been identified as a free black man. He was a slave owned by Winchester attorney Richard E. Byrd. Laws was being rented by Byrd to someone in Clarke County—a common practice in the Shenandoah Valley. For further discussion, see Jordan, *Black Confederates*, 285.

58. Sheridan, *Personal Memoirs*, 2:277–78.

59. "The Heroine of Winchester: How a Quaker Maiden Assisted Sheridan to Win the Battle," undated article in Philip H. Sheridan Papers.

60. Dannett, "Rebecca Wright," 105–7.

61. Miscellaneous article in Philip H. Sheridan Papers.

62. Sheridan to Wright, January 7, 1867, quoted in *New York Times*, July 28, 1912.

63. *New Hampshire Sentinel*, February 14, 1867.

64. *Olympia Record*, April 3, 1906.

65. *New York Times*, July 28, 1912.

66. Ibid.

67. *Winchester Times*, February 20, 1867.

68. *Detroit Post and Tribune*, "The Virginia Heroine," January 16, 1883, in Philip H. Sheridan Papers.

69. *New York Times*, February 26, 1867.

70. *Morning Star*, July 12, 1888.

71. Rebecca Wright to Charles Carleton Coffin, May 1, 1890, Houghton Library, Harvard University; *Morning Star*, July 12, 1888.

72. *Morning Star*, July 12, 1888.

73. *United States Treasury Register*, 41; *San Francisco Bulletin*, March 22, 1884.

74. Kinchen, *Women Who Spied for Blue and Gray*, 114–15. For a more in-depth examination of Wright's Unionism, her postwar dilemmas and how Sheridan helped her overcome them, see Noyalas, "'That Woman Was Worth a Whole Brigade,'" 43–49.

75. Neff, *Honoring the Civil War Dead*, 160–61.

76. Roland, *Reflections on Lee*, 119.

77. For further discussion on the construction of Lee's character by postwar writers, such as General Jubal A. Early, see Gary W. Gallagher, "Shaping Public Memory of the Civil War: Robert E. Lee, Jubal A. Early, and Douglas Southall Freeman," in Fahs and Waugh, *Memory of the Civil War*, 39–63. The adulation heaped on Lee after his death and portrayal of him as someone who favored reconciliation with the North greatly bothered some individuals, most notably Frederick Douglass. Douglass believed that all the praise Lee received in Northern newspapers proved improper to the memory of Union veterans and African Americans. Douglass informed a friend that the articles about Lee proved "nauseating." See Gallagher and Nolan, *Myth of the Lost Cause*, 44; Varon, *Appomattox*, 2–4, 188, 204.

78. Jones, *Personal Reminiscences*, 218; *Staunton Spectator and General Advertiser*, October 18, 1870.

79. Daniel, *Ceremonies*, 50.

80. According to census data for 1870, the population of African Americans decreased in the counties of Clarke, Frederick, Page, Rockbridge, Rockingham, Shenandoah and Warren from 1860 numbers. Census data reveals that there were 3,706 fewer African Americans in the Shenandoah Valley in 1870 as compared to 1860. See Koons, "The Colored Laborers Work as Well as When Slaves," in Geier and Potter, *Archaeological Perspectives*, 243.

81. Testimony of George Taylor, February 2, 1866, in *Report of the Joint Committee*, 40.

82. Ashby, *Valley Campaigns*, 108. Former Confederates used a variety of methods to prevent African Americans from realizing their freedom after the Civil War, hence the departure of great numbers in the immediate wake of the conflict. Among those things that former Confederates attempted to disrupt were efforts to educate African Americans who remained in the Shenandoah Valley after the conflict. For example, in February 1866, an anonymous individual from Shenandoah County sent a letter to the leader of the freedmen's school in the county and instructed him to shut

the school down and "leave or take the consequences." For further discussion, see Watkins James Testimony, February 12, 1866, in *Report of the Joint Committee*, 41. Exceptions, however, do exist. Some Shenandoah Valley residents hoped African Americans might remain in the region, become educated and become active participants in society. Among those who hoped to help African Americans make the transition was Sarah J. Percival, a resident of Winchester, who taught former slaves after the conflict. For further discussion of Percival's efforts, see Butchart, *Schooling the Freedpeople*, 65. For an analysis of this census data, see Kenneth E. Koons, "African Americans in the Breadbasket of the Confederacy," in Geier and Potter, *Archaeological Perspectives*, 242–43.

83. Berkey, "War in the Borderland," 272.
84. McConnell, *Glorious Contentment*, 24–27.
85. Ibid., 213, 215.
86. *History of the Easel Shaped Monument*, 397–98.
87. McConnel, *Glorious Contentment*, 215. Like most GAR posts in Virginia, the Mulligan Post has a history that is somewhat cloudy, but newspapers clearly show the Mulligan Post remained active for decades after its formation. For example, an article in the *Richmond Times-Dispatch* from May 28, 1916, states that Memorial Day activities in the Winchester National Cemetery were performed "under the auspices of Mulligan Post, GAR of Winchester."
88. Blair, *Cities of the Dead*, 121–23.
89. Ibid., 124–25.
90. Blight, *Race and Reunion*, 135.
91. Speech of Rutherford B. Hayes at Frederick County Agricultural Fair, October 16, 1878, Rutherford B. Hayes Papers.
92. Ibid.
93. Ibid.
94. *Staunton Spectator*, June 18, 1878; Blair, *Cities of the Dead*, 118.
95. *Winchester News*, February 14, 1879.
96. Morgan, *Address of Hon. Jno. T. Morgan*, 4.
97. Ibid.
98. Ibid.
99. Ibid., 9, 24. Addressing slavery as central in the coming of the conflict, Morgan stated: "African slavery was recognized and guaranteed...this was the view that the people of the South took of the subject."
100. *Southern Historical Society Papers* 8 (1880): 333–34. For further information on the Battle of Front Royal and the capture of Kenly's colors, see Cozzens, *Shenandoah 1862*, 294–307.
101. Toomey, *Hero at Front Royal*, 90.
102. "Note for Peace." For further discussion of Blue-Gray Reunions throughout the nation, see Blight, *Race and Reunion*, 201–5.
103. For further discussion of this sentiment, see Carol Reardon, "Binding the Wounds of War," in Logue and Barton, *Civil War Veteran*, 401–2.
104. Koons, "African Americans in the Breadbasket of the Confederacy," in Geier and Potter, *Archaeological Perspectives*, 241.

105. King and Derby, *Camp-Fire Sketches*, 513.
106. Silber, *Romance of Reunion*, 66–70.

CHAPTER 2

107. Buffum, *Sheridan's Veterans*, 9.
108. Ibid., 11.
109. Ibid., 10. For a brief biographical treatment of Carroll D. Wright, which largely focuses on his postwar life, see Leiby, *Carroll Wright*.
110. See Sibler, *Romance and Reunion*.
111. Registration form "Sheridan's Veterans: A Trip to the Shenandoah Valley, 1883," Sheridan's Veterans' Materials.
112. Ibid.
113. Ibid. For a complete roster of the 1883 excursion, see Appendix A.
114. Buffum, *Sheridan's Veterans*, 7.
115. "Sheridan's Veterans: Excursion to the Shenandoah Valley, September 15–25, 1883, Reunions and Camp Fires on Old Battle Fields, Plan of the Trip and Programme of Exercises," Sheridan's Veterans' Materials.
116. Whitney, *Union and Confederate Campaigns*, 1.
117. Allan, *History of the Campaign*.
118. Pond, *Shenandoah Valley in 1864*.
119. John Peyton Clark Papers, article copied into papers, April 18, 1862, HL.
120. Strader, *Civil War Journal*, 41. For additional discussion on this particular episode see Noyalas, *Stonewall Jackson's 1862 Valley Campaign*, 47.
121. Davidson, *Civil War Letters*, 31.
122. Coffin, *Freedom Triumphant*, 57–58.
123. In her diary on September 20, 1864, Mary Lee wrote, "They have not brought in…all of theirs and they will not allow any citizens to go to the field lest we should count their unburied dead." Strader, *Civil War Journal*, 417.
124. Resolution of the Winchester City Council, August 21, 1883, quoted in Buffum, *Sheridan's Veterans*, 22–23.
125. Testimony of Lewis T. Moore, Heater Claim Brief on Loyalty, Belle Grove Collection, Box 13, HL. For additional information on Moore see Robertson, *Stonewall Jackson*, 240. The members of the committee were as follows: Lewis T. Moore, Bentley Kern, Samuel R. Atwell, James B. Russell, A.M. Baker, E.H. Boyd, R.W. Hunter, John J. Williams, T.W. Harrison, Joseph A. Nulton, Charles H. Hoover, George S. Bushnell, James P. Riely, John H. Dean, C.M. Gibbons, Samuel L. Larew, Dr. William S. Miller, German Smith, J.J. Jordan, Charles W. Mensell, Henry Kinzell, Oscar Barr, Isaac H. Faulkner Jr. and William T. Gilbert. *Winchester News*, September 14, 1883.
126. *Winchester News*, September 14, 1883.
127. Ibid.
128. "Vale" to editor of the *Boston Daily Globe*, September 22, 1883, quoted in *Boston Daily Globe*, September 27, 1883.

129. Carroll D. Wright to Bentley Kern, September 1, 1883, quoted in Buffum, *Sheridan's Veterans*, 23.

130. Buffum, *Sheridan's Veterans*, 23.

131. "Sheridan's Veterans: A Trip to the Shenandoah Valley," Sheridan's Veterans Materials.

132. Buffum, *Sheridan's Veterans*, 12.

133. Ibid., 13.

134. The itinerary for the trip is derived from "Sheridan's Veterans...Plan of the Trip and Programme of Exercises," Sheridan's Veterans Materials.

135. During the Army of the Shenandoah's advance on Winchester on September 19, 1864, the Union Sixth Corps, commanded by General Horatio G. Wright, led the way, with Emory's command behind. Despite a directive from Sheridan, Wright had all his wagon trains follow his corps' advance. The presence of this rolling stock behind Wright's column and in front of Emory's delayed Emory tremendously. Frustrated, Emory decided to take his men off the Berryville Pike and advance them toward Winchester over rough terrain situated on the north side of the pike. After the battle, Union veteran John Mead Gould, an officer in Emory's command, recalled that the Army of the Shenandoah lost a "precious hour" and that the delay in arriving on the battlefield "was occasioned by the arrival of the 6th Corps and its trains, ammunition, and ambulances." Northern newspaper coverage of the delay at Winchester, however, placed all of the blame exclusively on General Emory. For example, two days after the battle, the *New York Tribune* reported: "There was a delay of at least two hours, caused by the non-arrival of the 19th Corps, who, through misconception of orders, had failed to come up at the proper time." Emory's battle for reputation continued after the conflict as well. In William Swinton's *Campaigns of the Army of the Potomac*, he placed all of the blame for Sheridan's delay on Emory's shoulders. *New York Tribune*, September 21, 1864; *Harper's Weekly*, October 8, 1864; Jordan, *Civil War Journals*, 397–99; Swinton, *Campaigns of the Army of the Potomac*, 557. For the most current treatment of the delay, see Patchan, *Last Battle of Winchester*, 229–31.

136. Buffum, *Sheridan's Veterans*, 13.

137. For the best overall treatment of military operations in the Shenandoah Valley, see Wert, *From Winchester to Cedar Creek*.

138. Buffum, *Sheridan's Veterans*, 15.

139. Ibid.

140. Ibid., 16.

141. *Spirit of Jefferson*, September 16, 1883.

142. Buffum, *Sheridan's Veterans*, 20.

143. "Sheridan's Veterans...Plan of the Trip and Programme of Exercises," Sheridan's Veterans Materials.

144. Buffum, *Sheridan's Veterans*, 21.

145. Ibid., 22.

146. Ibid.

147. *Spirit of Jefferson*, September 25, 1883.

148. Buffum, *Sheridan's Veterans*, 23.

149. Ibid.

150. Address of Mayor William Clark, September 18, 1883, quoted in Buffum, *Sheridan's Veterans*, 24.

151. Ibid., 25.

152. Ibid.

153. Speech of Colonel Carroll D. Wright, September 18, 1883, quoted in Buffum, *Sheridan's Veterans*, 27.

154. Blight, *Race and Reunion*, 218–19.

155. Buffum, *Sheridan's Veterans*, 28.

156. Ibid., 29.

157. Address of Sergeant Ransom Huntoon, September 19, 1883, quoted in Buffum, *Sheridan's Veterans*, 33.

158. Address of Colonel Carroll D. Wright at Camp Emory, September 19, 1883, quoted in Buffum, *Sheridan's Veterans*, 50.

159. Address of Captain Charles P. Hall, Winchester National Cemetery, September 19, 1883, quoted in Buffum, *Sheridan's Veterans*, 57–58.

160. Address of General William H. Emory, Winchester National Cemetery, September 19, 1883, quoted in Buffum, *Sheridan's Veterans*, 62.

161. Ibid.

162. Rhodes, *All for the Union*, 181.

163. Address of Colonel Carroll D. Wright, Stonewall Confederate Cemetery, September 19, 1883, quoted in Buffum, *Sheridan's Veterans*, 63.

164. For a brief biographical treatment of Coffin, see Schildt, *Charles Carleton Coffin*, 3–6.

165. Charles C. Coffin, account of ceremony in Stonewall Confederate Cemetery, September 19, 1883, quoted in Buffum, *Sheridan's Veterans*, 64–65.

166. For further discussion of Union soldiers participating in ceremonies to honor Confederates, see Blair, *Cities of the Dead*, 154–61.

167. Charles C. Coffin, account of ceremony in Stonewall Confederate Cemetery, September 19, 1883, quoted in Buffum, *Sheridan's Veterans*, 64–65.

168. *Winchester News*, September 21, 1883.

169. Ibid.

170. Buffum, *Sheridan's Veterans*, 88.

171. Address of General William H. Emory, September 22, 1883, Camp Emory, Winchester, quoted in Buffum, *Sheridan's Veterans*, 96.

172. Ibid.

173. Address of Colonel Carroll D. Wright on the departure from Winchester, September 22, 1883, quoted in Buffum, *Sheridan's Veterans*, 98.

174. Ibid.

175. Address of Mayor Clark, September 22, 1883, quoted in Buffum, *Sheridan's Veterans*, 101.

176. Ibid., 103.

177. Wayland, *History of Rockingham County*, 174.

178. Buffum, *Sheridan's Veterans*, 110.

179. "Obituary of Colonel D.H. Lee Martz," 82.

180. Buffum, *Sheridan's Veterans*, 106.
181. *Spirit of Jefferson*, September 25, 1883.
182. Address of Samuel J. Harnsberger, September 22, 1883, Harrisonburg, quoted in Buffum, *Sheridan's Veterans*, 108.
183. Buffum, *Sheridan's Veterans*, 108.
184. For further discussion of Union wartime admiration for Stonewall Jackson, see Gallagher, *Lee and His Generals*, 104–5; Garner, *Civil War World of Herman Melville*, 242–43; Rable, *God's Almost Chosen Peoples*, 260–64.
185. Address of Carroll D. Wright, September 22, 1883, Harrisonburg, quoted in Buffum, *Sheridan's Veterans*, 109–10.
186. Buffum, *Sheridan's Veterans*, 112.
187. Ibid.
188. Ibid., 110–11.
189. Address of General Elisha Hunt Rhodes, September 23, 1883, quoted in Buffum, *Sheridan's Veterans*, 113.
190. Buffum, *Sheridan's Veterans*, 114.
191. Observations of Joshua M. Addeman, quoted in Buffum, *Sheridan's Veterans*, 114–15.
192. *Winchester News*, September 21, 1883.
193. Unidentified resident of Winchester quoted in *Boston Daily Globe*, September 27, 1883.
194. Although many Union veterans embraced the spirit of reconciliation, some did not. Aside from those who desired to maintain the legacy of emancipation, some Union veterans refused to reconcile with former Confederates due to the horrible treatment perpetrated by Confederates on Union prisoners of war. For more on this discussion, see Cloyd, *Haunted by Atrocity*, 56–58.

CHAPTER 3

195. Buffum, *Sheridan's Veterans*, 89.
196. Ibid., *Sheridan's Veterans No. II*, 115.
197. *Boston Journal*, December 11, 1884.
198. *Boston Daily Globe*, September 18, 1885.
199. Buffum, *Sheridan's Veterans No. II*, 8–9.
200. Ibid., 9.
201. "Fourteenth New Hampshire Annual Reunion, 1885, on the Battlefield of the Opequon, September 19," regimental circular, Fourteenth New Hampshire Veterans' Materials.
202. *Winchester Times*, August 26, 1885.
203. *Winchester News* article quoted in Buffum, *Sheridan's Veterans No. II*, 16.
204. *Boston Daily Globe*, September 19, 1885.
205. For further discussion of the reaction to Grant's death in the South, Grant's funeral procession and the role played by veterans of the Stonewall Brigade and its band, see Waugh, *U.S. Grant*, 232–41, and Brice, *Stonewall Brigade Band*, 81.

At the request of Julia Dent Grant, two former Confederate generals—Joseph E. Johnston and Simon Bolivar Buckner—served as honorary pallbearers for Grant's funeral. For further discussion, see Flood, *Grant's Final Victory*, 231.

206. Buffum, *Sheridan's Veterans No. II*, 17.

207. Ibid.

208. Ibid.

209. *Boston Daily Globe*, September 14, 1885.

210. Ibid.

211. *Winchester Times*, September 16, 1885.

212. Ibid.

213. This number includes civilian participants in the excursion as well. For a complete listing of the attendees at the 1885 reunion, see Appendix B.

214. *Boston Daily Globe*, September 27, 1885.

215. Ibid.

216. Ibid.

217. Ibid.

218. Ibid., September 23, 1885; Buffum, *Sheridan's Veterans No. II*, 16.

219. Jones, *Virginia's Next Governor*, 26–27.

220. Ibid., 27.

221. Ibid.

222. *Baltimore Sun*, September 19, 1885.

223. Letter of Fitzhugh Lee to SVA, quoted in *Winchester Times*, September 23, 1885.

224. *Winchester Times*, September 18, 1885.

225. Buffum, *Sheridan's Veterans No. II*, 25.

226. *Boston Daily Globe*, September 19, 1885.

227. Letter of unidentified female resident of Harrisonburg to sister in Lynchburg, quoted in Buffum, *Sheridan's Veterans No. II*, 36–37.

228. Ibid., 39.

229. For further discussion on the significance of former Confederate women as the guardians of Confederate dead and heritage, see Janney, *Burying the Dead*. Another item that became apparent to Union veterans after 1895 and the creation of the United Daughters of the Confederacy was that women played a vital role in the flow of knowledge and crafting the war's history for children. For further discussion, see James M. McPherson, "Long-Legged Yankee Lies: The Lost Cause Textbook Crusade," in McPherson, *This Mighty Scourge*, 93–106, and Carol Reardon, "William T. Sherman in Postwar Georgia's Collective Memory, 1864–1914," in Waugh and Gallagher, *Wars Within a War*, 240–41.

230. For general discussions of the reverence for Confederate dead, see Neff, *Honoring the Civil War Dead*, 176.

231. *Boston Daily Globe*, September 27, 1885.

232. The monument around which Sheridan's Veterans gathered in 1885 was dedicated in 1876. Sedore, *Illustrated Guide*, 51–52.

233. *Boston Daily Globe*, September 19, 1885.

234. Buffum, *Sheridan's Veterans No. II*, 35.

235. Ibid.

236. Sedore, *Illustrated Guide*, 52.

237. Buffum, *Sheridan's Veterans No. II*, 35.

238. Ibid., 37–38.

239. Ibid., 38.

240. Remarks of Judge John Paul, Harrisonburg, September 18, 1885, quoted in *Boston Daily Globe*, September 19, 1885.

241. Buffum, *Sheridan's Veterans No. II*, 41.

242. *Winchester Times*, September 23, 1885. The Gray rifle team won a special trophy created for the occasion. Francis Buffum described it as follows: "It consists of a perfect small cannon of solid, silver, the barrel being plated with gold. Every part of the gun carriage, appurtenances, etc. is perfect and complete, while a shield of silver, leaning against the carriage, contains the inscription. This unique piece of artillery stands on a mound of silver imitative of earth, and the gun is unlimbered, ready for action." See Buffum, *Sheridan's Veterans No. II*, 74. An article published after the competition by a Union veteran stated that it was actually the Blue team that won the match by a score of 56 to 46. Union veteran Donald C. Ball of the First Michigan Cavalry wrote that there was a "rifle competition between picked blue and grey teams. The match was won by the blue team 56 to 46 before a large and intensely interested crowd." References from Francis Buffum, the excursion's historian, clearly state that the Gray team won the match. See "Rifle Matches for Veterans."

243. Buffum, *Sheridan's Veterans No. II*, 42; *Spirit of Jefferson*, September 22, 1885.

244. Buffum, *Sheridan's Veterans No. II*, 43.

245. Unidentified former Confederate woman's perspective on the Union reunion in Harrisonburg, September 18, 1885, quoted in *Sheridan's Veterans No. II*, 34.

246. *Baltimore Sun*, September 19, 1885.

247. Buffum, *Sheridan's Veterans No. II*, 47.

248. Ibid., 46–47.

249. Ibid., 44.

250. Ibid., 73.

251. Rogers, *Everlasting Glory*, 54.

252. For more on the Eighth Vermont's actions at Winchester, see Wert, *From Winchester to Cedar Creek*, 62–63.

253. Eighth Vermont dedication speech of Colonel Herbert E. Hill, read by Colonel John B. Mead, September 19, 1885, quoted in Buffum, *Sheridan's Veterans No. II*, 57.

254. Ibid., 61.

255. W.H. Gimore, State of Vermont Quartermaster General's Office to Dept. Quartermaster, Washington, D.C., December 13, 1895, copy of letter in author's possession.

256. Charles Carleton Coffin speech, September 19, 1885, quoted in Buffum, *Sheridan's Veterans No. II*, 66–69.

257. Ibid., 117.

258. Ibid., 74–75.

259. *Winchester Times*, September 23, 1885.

260. Ibid.
261. Ibid.
262. Buffum, *Sheridan's Veterans No. II*, 86.
263. Ibid. The following members of the SVA took part in the re-created Sheridan's Ride: Colonel A.C. Wellington, Major E.L. Noyes, Captain J.W. Hervey, Captain E.D. Hadley, Sergeant R.E. Schouler, Sergeant Lyman Aylesworth, Lieutenant F.C. Forbes, Sergeant L.K. Stiles, George Cushman, R.W. Randall and Captain F.H. Buffum.
264. For further discussion on the stand of Thomas's brigade and the fate of the Eighth Vermont at Cedar Creek, see Noyalas, *Battle of Cedar Creek*, 43–45; Carpenter, *History of the Eighth Vermont*, 209–12; Rogers, *Everlasting Glory*, 55.
265. Buffum, *Sheridan's Veterans No. II*, 88–89.
266. Ibid., 92.
267. Ibid., 99.
268. Ibid., 95.
269. Ibid., 100.
270. Ibid.
271. Geier and Hardin, *Overview and Assessment*, 262–63.
272. Buffum, *Sheridan's Veterans No. II*, 100.
273. Ibid., 101.
274. Ibid., 119.
275. *Boston Daily Globe*, September 24, 1885.

CHAPTER 4

276. Ibid, September 21, 1886.
277. Ibid.
278. Ibid.
279. Ibid.
280. *Valley Virginian*, October 27, 1870.
281. *Omaha Daily Bee*, November 23, 1886.
282. *Shenandoah Herald*, November 19, 1886. In the newspaper article, it states that Sheridan arrived on "Monday of this week," which, in 1886, was November 15.
283. Ibid., November 19, 1864.
284. Ibid.
285. *Staunton Spectator*, June 15, 1887. The exchanges between Fitzhugh Lee and William Averell are not surprising. When Lee won his bid for governor of Virginia in 1885, Averell penned a note to Lee expressing his congratulation. Averell wrote, "Accept my hearty congratulations. I shall rejoice in your election." See Jones, *Virginia's Next Governor*, 28.
286. *Staunton Spectator*, June 8, 1887.
287. Ewer, *Third Massachusetts Cavalry*, 378.
288. *Philadelphia Inquirer*, September 20, 1888.
289. Remington Hepburn target rifle.

290. Unmarked newspaper clipping, "3ʳᵈ Massachusetts Cavalry Visit to Shenandoah Valley, 1888," Jonathan A. Noyalas.
291. Foster, *Ghosts of the Confederacy*, 55, 71.
292. *Columbus Daily Enquirer*, June 7, 1889.
293. *Spirit of Jefferson*, June 18, 1889.
294. *Wichita Daily Eagle*, June 14, 1889.
295. *Manning Times*, June 12, 1889. Historian Gaines M. Foster noted that by the end of the 1880s, unreconstructed Confederates, such as Early, were in a clear minority. While they might have been tolerated out of respect for the previous Confederate service, these men stood on the margins. See Foster, *Ghosts of the Confederacy*, 71.
296. *Boston Journal*, August 28, 1889.
297. Program, Twenty-second Annual Reunion, 114ᵗʰ New York Regimental Association, Winchester, Virginia, September 19, 1864–94, Jonathan A. Noyalas.
298. *Columbus Daily Enquirer*, June 7, 1889.
299. Janney, *Remembering the Civil War*, 180.
300. Steele and Steele, *Brief History*, 264–65.
301. Mallin and Radi, *Ashby Camp*, 33. The Turner Ashby Camp was officially established on September 28, 1891.
302. Address of Governor Urban A. Woodbury, September 20, 1895, quoted in Smith, *Chickamauga Memorial*, 62.
303. Ibid.; Mallin and Radi, *Ashby Camp*, 34.
304. *Springfield Republican*, October 10, 1895.
305. *Morning Herald*, October 10, 1896; *Boston Journal*, October 9, 1896.
306. *Morning Herald*, October 10, 1896.
307. Confederate Veterans of the Valley Circular, quoted in Mallin and Radi, *Ashby Camp*, 46.
308. Ibid.
309. Blight, *Beyond the Battlefield*, 103.
310. *Shenandoah Valley-Supplement*, May 20, 1897.
311. Ibid.
312. Mallin and Radi, *Ashby Camp*, 51.
313. In the records of the Ashby Camp, the two individuals who disagreed about using the American flag are identified as Murray and Boyd. There were three members of the Ashby camp with the last name Boyd. Dr. Philip W. Boyd Sr., who served with Captain R. Preston Chew's Battery; Sergeant John Elisha Boyd Jr., who served with the First Virginia Cavalry; and Lieutenant Elisha Holmes Boyd, who served in the Rockbridge Artillery. There was only one member of the camp with the last name Murray, J. Ogden Murray, who served in the Seventh Virginia Cavalry. See Mallin and Radi, *Ashby Camp*, 52, 131, 135. Like every aspect of postwar reconciliation, outliers existed among both Union and Confederate veterans. For further discussion of Confederate veterans who did not want to support the American cause in the conflict with Spain, see Janney, *Remembering the Civil War*, 222–31. For additional perspectives on the role of the Spanish-American War in helping further advance the cause of reconciliation, see Marten, *Sing Not War*, 23, and Blight, *Race and Reunion*, 351–53.

314. Curtis, *Proceedings of the Twenty-Sixth Annual Reunion*, 15–16.

315. For further discussion on divisions among Union veterans' attitudes on the use and display of the Confederate flag after the dedication of the Lee equestrian statue in Richmond, see Blair, *Cities of the Dead*, 154–58. While the dedication of the Lee equestrian statue marked the first significant display of Confederate flags after the conflict, the first appearance of Confederate flags in the Shenandoah Valley seems to be June 1887 during a memorial honoring Union and Confederate veterans in Staunton, Virginia. A correspondent for the *Staunton Spectator* wrote on June 15, 1887, "The Blue and the Gray! National and Confederate Flags Blended in Token of Peace and Friendship."

316. Curtis, *Proceedings of the Twenty-Sixth Annual Reunion*, 21–22. For further discussion about the complexities of the display of the Confederate flag and its evolution of meaning since the Civil War's end, see Coski, *Confederate Flag*.

317. Curtis, *Proceedings of the Twenty-Sixth Annual Reunion*, 35.

318. Ibid., 36.

319. "Twenty-Sixth Annual Reunion of the 114th Regimental Association and Dedication of the State Monument at Winchester, Virginia, October Nineteenth, 1898," program in Philip Williams Family Papers.

320. Curtis, *Proceedings of the Twenty-Sixth Annual Reunion*, 57.

321. Ibid., 61.

322. Ibid.

323. Ibid., 57, 64.

324. Wright, "Old Farm-House," 225; Marten, *Sing Not War*, 273.

CHAPTER 5

325. Blight, *Race and Reunion*, 351.

326. McClure and Morris, *Authentic Life*, 193.

327. *Duluth News-Tribune*, May 21, 1899.

328. Ibid.

329. Ibid.

330. *Philadelphia Inquirer*, May 22, 1899.

331. Carmichael, *Last Generation*, 232.

332. Mallin and Radi, *Ashby Camp*, 66.

333. Ibid., 73; Blight, *Race and Reunion*, 352. According to Blight, by 1900, 128 Confederate dead were reinterred in Arlington National Cemetery, with the first Confederate Memorial Day being observed at Arlington three years later.

334. The veterans of the Fifty-fourth Pennsylvania invited the Ashby Camp to Johnstown due to the warm welcome the Pennsylvanians received when they visited the Shenandoah Valley in October 1903. For more discussion of this reunion, see Mallin and Radi, *Ashby Camp*, 96, 102.

335. *Evening Star*, October 7, 1904, quoted in Mallin and Radi, *Ashby Camp*, 105.

336. For the best treatment of the Battle of New Market, see Knight, *Valley Thunder*.

337. *Rockingham Register*, June 27, 1905 article clipping in Fifty-fourth Pennsylvania Monument File.

338. *Shenandoah Valley*, August 10, 1905, newspaper clipping in Fifty-fourth Pennsylvania Monument File. For further discussion of the destruction endured by Shenandoah County residents during Sheridan's Burning in late September and early October 1864, see Heatwole, *Burning*, 135–212.

339. *Rockingham Register*, October 27, 1905, newspaper clipping in Fifty-fourth Pennsylvania Monument File.

340. Ibid.; Charles R. Knight, in his study of the Battle of New Market, noted that six years after the monument's dedication, the Fifty-fourth Pennsylvania's veterans returned to the Shenandoah Valley for a reunion. In preparation for the reunion, a veteran of the regiment corresponded with a Confederate veteran in the Shenandoah Valley and wrote, "I think it is safe for me to say there is very little, if any, harsh feeling toward those we met there on the 15th of May 1864." While this comment illustrates a fading of ill will toward Confederate veterans and vice versa, it does not indicate that Union or Confederate veterans were willing to admit that their respective armies did anything wrong during the conflict. See Knight, *Valley Thunder*, 268.

341. *Pilgrimage of the Fifteenth*, 33.

342. Gold, *History of Clarke County Virginia*, 319–20.

343. *Pilgrimage of the Fifteenth*, 36.

344. *Exercises at the Dedication of a Monument*, 4.

345. Ibid., 5–6.

346. Speech of Herbert S. Larrick, quoted in *Exercises at the Dedication of a Monument*, 11–15; *Evening Enterprise*, October 12, 1907.

347. *Baltimore Sun*, August 8, 1909.

348. Ibid., August 7, 1910.

349. Ibid.

350. Morton, *Story of Winchester*, 250.

351. Davis, *Shenandoah*, 316.

352. Colt, *Defend the Valley*, 402–3.

353. Buck, *With the Old Confeds*, 137–38.

354. Colt, *Defend the Valley*, 402–3. Barton had two sons who fought in World War I. David Barton served in the 110th Field Artillery, 29th Infantry Division, and Alexander Barton served in the 149th Field Artillery, 42nd Infantry Division.

355. Mallin and Radi, *Ashby Camp*, 127.

356. Cartmell, *Shenandoah Valley Pioneers*, 443; inscription on tombstone of Joseph A. Potts, Mount Hebron Cemetery, Winchester, Virginia.

357. "Program for the Dedication of the Ramseur Monument," Monuments and Memorials Collection.

358. DuPont, *Address by Colonel DuPont*, 1, 14. For further discussion of the circumstances of Ramseur's wounding and death, see Gallagher, *Stephen Dodson Ramseur*, 164–68, and Kundahl, *Bravest of the Brave*, 290–305.

359. Mallin and Radi, *Ashby Camp*, 125; Ashby, *Valley Campaigns*, 326.

360. *Evening Star*, May 30, 1936, quoted in Mallin and Radi, *Ashby Camp*, 129. Dellinger died on August 29, 1943, and is believed to be the last surviving Confederate veteran from the lower Shenandoah Valley.

361. *Pilgrimage of the Fifteenth*, 56.

362. Lincoln's second inaugural quoted in Basler, *Collected Works*, 8:332.

363. *Pilgrimage of the Fifteenth*, 40. This perspective challenges the thesis of David Blight's *Race and Reunion*. For other examples that challenge the idea that veterans, particularly Union veterans, abandoned their views on the Civil War or refused to address the idea that they fought for right, see Gannon, *Won Cause*, 164–65; Janney, *Remembering the Civil War*; Janney, "No 'Sickly Sentimental Gush," in Jones and Sword, *Gateway to the Confederacy*, 285–309.

EPILOGUE

364. *Winchester Times*, September 23, 1885.

365. The charred wheat came from the Humbert-Knightly Mill in Augusta County. Garber and Harner, *History New Hope*, 51–52.

366. There is no denying the fact that the Civil War centennial had a pageant-like quality to it. Despite the efforts discussed in this epilogue to show that a few reasonable attempts were made to rekindle some of the efforts of the veterans and show respect for both sides, the centennial commemorations in the Shenandoah Valley contained a significant amount of theater intended to romanticize the conflict. For example, in late April 1961, the organizers of the Shenandoah Apple Blossom festival held in Winchester on April 27–28 presented "A Colorful Civil War Centennial Pageant of Springtime" based on the Civil War diary of Mary Greenhow Lee. See "Thirty-fourth Annual Apple Blossom Program," Civil War Centennial Materials. For further discussion of the pageant-like quality of the Civil War centennial commemorations, see Cook, *Troubled Commemoration*, 15–50. By the end of the centennial, the organizers of the Apple Blossom Festival gave a slight nod to reconciliation with the choice of cover art for the program. The organizers of Winchester's thirty-eighth annual Apple Blossom Festival, held on April 29–May 1, 1965, chose as the cover art for the festival program an oil painting entitled *Miss Traveler-Teen*. Clad in an outfit of half Union blue, half Confederate gray, with a belt adorned by two buckles—one engraved with "CSA," the other with "USA"—the girl in the painting evoked a sense of respect for veterans of both armies.

367. "Souvenir Program Re-Activated Battle of Fisher's Hill, Va., August 5, 1961," Civil War Centennial Materials.

368. Leekley, *Bruce Catton*, 3.

369. Bruce Catton observation in Webb, *Crucial Moments*, 7.

370. During the Civil War centennial, eminent historian John Hope Franklin seethed with anger over how the centennial in 1962—the 100th anniversary of Lincoln's preliminary Emancipation Proclamation—failed to bring African Americans into the various commemorative efforts. "While the war is over," Franklin penned,

"the battle to free man's mind and his actions of hatred and racial bigotry has not been won." Franklin, "Century of Civil War Observance," 107.

Franklin's frustration regarding the exclusion of the African American story during the centennial was undoubtedly compounded by inaccurate portrayals of African Americans during the conflict—chief among them the myth of the happy slave. In the Shenandoah Valley, the most controversial monument meant to promulgate the myth of the happy slave is the monument to Heyward Shepherd erected in Harpers Ferry under the auspices of the United Daughters of the Confederacy in October 1931. The monument commemorates the mortal wounding of Shepherd, a baggage-handler on the Baltimore & Ohio Railroad who became the first casualty in John Brown's raid on Harpers Ferry in October 1859. Instead of portraying Shepherd as an innocent bystander shot accidentally, the monument conveys a sense that Shepherd attempted to stop Brown's raid on Harpers Ferry and thus his attempt to begin a campaign to destroy slavery throughout the South. Implied in the language is that Shepherd, a free black from Winchester, approved of slavery and sacrificed his life to protect it.

For further discussion, see Edward T. Lilenthal, "Heritage and History: The Dilemmas of Interpretation," in Sutton, *Rally on the High Ground*, 37–43.

371. On the problem of presentism in historical judgment, see Roland, *History Teaches Us to Hope*, 41, and David W. Blight, "Healing and History: Battlefields and the Problem of Civil War Memory," in Sutton, *Rally on the High Ground*, 24.

372. Buffum, *Sheridan's Veterans No II*, 39.

APPENDIX A

373. The 1883 roster is derived from Buffum, *Sheridan's Veterans*, 121–28.

APPENDIX B

374. The 1885 roster is derived from Buffum, *Sheridan's Veterans No. II*, 121–28.

BIBLIOGRAPHY

MANUSCRIPT COLLECTIONS

Belle Grove Collection; John Peyton Clark Papers; Mrs. Hugh Lee Collection; Philip Williams Family Papers; Turner Ashby Camp Papers. Stewart Bell Jr. Archives, Handley Regional Library, Winchester, Virginia.

Fifty-fourth Pennsylvania Monument File. Virginia Museum of the Civil War and New Market State Battlefield Historical Park, New Market, Virginia.

Fourteenth New Hampshire Veterans' Materials. Christopher Jordan, Kabletown, West Virginia.

Monuments and Memorials Collection. Eleanor S. Brockenbrough Library, Museum of the Confederacy, Richmond, Virginia.

114th New York Regimental Association Materials; Civil War Centennial Materials; Sheridan's Veterans' Materials. Jonathan A. Noyalas, Martinsburg, West Virginia.

Philip H. Sheridan Papers, Reel No. 94. Library of Congress, Washington, D.C.

Rebecca Wright to Charles Carleton Coffin, May 1, 1890. Houghton Library, Harvard University, Cambridge, Massachusetts.

Remington Hepburn Target Rifle, Stonewall Jackson's Headquarters Museum, Winchester, Virginia.

Rutherford B. Hayes Papers. Rutherford B. Hayes' Presidential Center, Fremont, Ohio.

Sheridan's Veterans' Materials. Nicholas P. Picerno, Bridgewater, Virginia.

Southern Claims Commission Reports, M1407. National Archives and Records Administration, Washington, D.C.

PUBLISHED PRIMARY SOURCES

Allan, William. *History of the Campaign of Gen. T.J. (Stonewall) Jackson in the Shenandoah Valley of Virginia, From November 4, 1861, to June 17, 1862.* Philadelphia: J.B. Lippincott, 1880.

Ashby, Thomas A. *The Valley Campaigns: Being the Reminiscences of a Non-Combatant While Between the Lines in the Shenandoah Valley during the War of the States.* New York: Neale Publishing Co., 1914.

Avirett, James B. *The Memoirs of General Turner Ashby and His Compeers.* Baltimore, MD: Selby and Dulany, 1867.

Basler, Roy P., ed. *The Collected Works of Abraham Lincoln.* Vols. 7 and 8. New Brunswick, NJ: Rutgers University Press, 1953.

Buck, Samuel P. *With the Old Confeds: Actual Experiences of a Captain in the Line.* Baltimore, MD: H.E. Houck & Co., 1925.

Buffum, Francis H. *Sheridan's Veterans Number II: A Souvenir of Their Third Campaign in the Shenandoah Valley, 1864, 1883, 1885.* Boston. W.F. Brown & Co., 1886.

————. *Sheridan's Veterans: A Souvenir of Their Two Campaigns in the Shenandoah Valley, The One, of War, in 1864, The Other of Peace, in 1883, Being the Record of the Excursion to the Battle-Fields of the Valley of Virginia, September 15–24, 1883.* Boston: W.F. Brown & Co., 1883.

Carpenter, George N. *History of the Eighth Vermont Volunteers, 1861–1865.* Boston: Press of Deland and Barta, 1886.

Casler, John O. *Four Years in the Stonewall Brigade.* Girard, KS: Appeal Publishing Co., 1906.

Colt, Margaretta Barton. *Defend the Valley: A Shenandoah Family in the Civil War.* Oxford, UK: Oxford University Press, 1994.

Curtis, O.H., comp. *Proceedings of the Twenty-Sixth Annual Reunion of the 114th N.Y. Regimental Association and Dedicatory Services at Winchester, VA., October 19, 1898.* Washington, D.C.: Conwell Print, 1899.

Daniel, John W. *Ceremonies Connected with the Inauguration of the Mausoleum and the Unveiling of the Recumbent Figure of General Robert Lee at Washington and Lee University, Lexington, Va., June 28, 1883: Historical Sketch of the Lee Memorial Association.* Richmond, VA: West, Johnson, and Co., 1883.

Davidson, Garber A., ed. *The Civil War Letters of the Late 1st Lieut. James J. Hartley, 122nd Ohio Infantry Regiment.* Jefferson, NC: McFarland, 1998.

Douglas, Henry Kyd. *I Rode with Stonewall.* Chapel Hill: University of North Carolina Press, 1940.

DuPont, Henry A. *Address by Colonel DuPont Upon the Unveiling of Major General Ramseur's Monument.* Winterthur, DE: H.A. DuPont, 1920.

Ewer, James K. *The Third Massachusetts Cavalry in the War for the Union.* N.p.: published by the direction of the Historical Committee of the Regimental Association, 1903.

Exercises at the Dedication of a Monument Erected on the Battlefield at Cedar Creek, Virginia by the Survivors of the 128th Regiment, N.Y.S.V.I., October 15, 1907. N.p.: published by the Committee, 1915.

BIBLIOGRAPHY

Jones, J. William. *Virginia's Next Governor: Gen'l. Fitzhugh Lee.* New York: Cheap Publishing Co., 1885.

Jones, John William. *Personal Reminiscences, Anecdotes, and Letters of General Robert E. Lee.* New York: D. Appleton & Co., 1874.

Jordan, William B., ed. *The Civil War Journals of John Mead Gould.* Baltimore, MD: Butternut and Blue, 1997.

King, W.C., and W.P. Derby, comps. *Camp-Fire Sketches and Battlefield Echoes.* Springfield, MA: King, Richardson, and Co., 1896.

Kundahl, George W., ed. *The Bravest of the Brave: The Correspondence of Stephen Dodson Ramseur.* Chapel Hill: University of North Carolina Press, 2010.

Morgan, John T. *Address of Hon. Jno. T. Morgan on the Unveiling of the Monuments to the Unknown Confederate Dead, Delivered at Winchester, Virginia, June 6th, 1879.* Washington, D.C.: Globe Printing and Publishing House, 1879.

"A Note for Peace: Reunions of the 'Blue and the Gray.'" *Century Magazine* 36, no. 3 (1888): 440–41.

"Obituary of Colonel D.H. Lee Martz." *Confederate Veteran* 23, no. 2 (February 1915): 82.

Opie, John N. *A Rebel Cavalryman.* Chicago: W.B. Conkey, 1899.

Pilgrimage of the Fifteenth New Jersey Volunteers' Veteran Association to Gettysburg and the Shenandoah Valley, May 21st to 25th, 1907. Elizabeth, NJ: Henry Cook Printshop, 1907.

Pollard, Edward A. *Southern History of the War: The Last Year of the War.* New York: Charles B. Richardson, 1866.

Report on the Joint Committee on Reconstruction at the First Session of the Thirty-Ninth Congress. Washington, D.C.: Government Printing Office, 1866.

Rhodes, Robert Hunt, ed. *All for the Union: The Civil War Diary and Letters of Elisha Hunt Rhodes.* New York: Vintage Books, 1985.

"Rifle Matches for Veterans." *Rifle* (May 1885).

Sheridan, Philip H. *Personal Memoirs of P.H. Sheridan.* 2 vols. New York: Charles L. Webster & Co., 1888.

Southern Historical Society Papers. 52 vols. Richmond, VA: Southern Historical Society, 1876–1952.

Strader, Eloise C., ed. *The Civil War Journal of Mary Greenhow Lee.* Winchester, VA: Winchester-Frederick County Historical Society, 2011.

Taylor, James E. *With Sheridan Up the Shenandoah Valley in 1864: Leaves from a Special Artists Sketch Book and Diary.* Dayton, OH: Morningside House, 1989.

Trowbridge, J.T. *The South: A Tour of Its Battle-Fields and Ruined Cities, A Journey through the Desolated States, and Talks with the People.* Hartford, CT: L. Stebbins, 1866.

Wenger, Norman R., and David S. Rodes. *Unionists and the Civil War Experience in the Shenandoah Valley.* Vol. 2. Dayton, VA: Valley Brethren-Mennonite Heritage Center, 2004.

Whitney, William H. *Union and Confederate Campaigns in the Lower Shenandoah Valley Illustrated: Twenty Years After at the First Reunion of Sheridan's Veterans on the Fields and in the Camps of the Valley.* Boston: W.H. Whitney, 1883.

Wright, Emma Howard. "The Old Farm-House at North Mountain." *Blue and Gray: The Patriotic American Magazine* (March 1893): 223–25.

BIBLIOGRAPHY

NEWSPAPERS

Baltimore Sun
Boston Daily Globe
Boston Journal
Columbus Daily Enquirer
Detroit Post and Tribune
Duluth News-Tribune
Evening Enterprise
Evening Star
Harper's Weekly
Manning Times
Morning Herald
Morning Star
New Hampshire Sentinel
New York Herald
New York Times
New York Tribune
Olympia Record

Omaha Daily Bee
Philadelphia Inquirer
Philadelphia Ledger
Rockingham Register
San Francisco Bulletin
Shenandoah Herald
Shenandoah Valley
Shenandoah Valley-Supplement
Spirit of Jefferson
Springfield Republican
Staunton Spectator
Staunton Spectator and General Advertiser
Valley Virginian
Wichita Daily Eagle
Winchester Journal
Winchester News
Winchester Times

SECONDARY SOURCES

Blair, William. *Cities of the Dead: Contesting the Memory of the Civil War in the South: 1861–1914*. Chapel Hill: University of North Carolina Press, 2004.

Blight, David W. *Beyond the Battlefield: Race, Memory, and the American Civil War*. Amherst: University of Massachusetts Press, 2002.

———. *Race and Reunion: The Civil War in American Memory*. Cambridge, MA: Belknap Press, 2001.

Brady, Lisa M. *War Upon the Land: Military Strategy and the Transformation of Southern Landscapes During the American Civil War*. Athens: University of Georgia Press, 2012.

Brice, Marshall Moore. *The Stonewall Brigade Band*. Verona, VA: McClure Printing, 1967.

Butchart, Ronald E. *Schooling the Freedpeople: Teaching, Learning, and the Struggle for Black Freedom, 1861–1876*. Chapel Hill: University of North Carolina Press, 2010.

Carmichael, Peter S. *The Last Generation: Young Virginians in Peace, War, and Reunion*. Chapel Hill: University of North Carolina Press, 2005.

Cartmell, Thomas K. *Shenandoah Valley Pioneers and Their Descendants: A History of Frederick County, Virginia*. Baltimore, MD: Chesapeake Book Co., 1963.

Cloyd, Benjamin C. *Haunted by Atrocity: Civil War Prisons in American Memory*. Baton Rouge: Louisiana State University Press, 2010.

Coffin, Charles Carleton. *Freedom Triumphant: The Fourth Period of the War of the Rebellion*. New York: Harper & Brothers, 1890.

BIBLIOGRAPHY

Cook, Robert J. *Troubled Commemoration: The American Civil War Centennial, 1961–1965*. Baton Rouge: Louisiana State University Press, 2007.

Coski, John M. *The Confederate Flag: America's Most Embattled Emblem*. Cambridge, MA: Belknap Press, 2005.

Cozzens, Peter. *Shenandoah 1862: Stonewall Jackson's 1862 Valley Campaign*. Chapel Hill: University of North Carolina Press, 2008.

Dannett, Sylvia G. "Rebecca Wright: Traitor or Patriot?" *Lincoln Herald* 69, no. 3 (1963): 103–12.

Davis, Julia. *Shenandoah*. New York: Rinehart & Co., 1945.

Duncan, Richard R. *Beleaguered Winchester: A Virginia Community at War, 1861–1865*. Baton Rouge: Louisiana State University Press, 2007.

Fahs, Alice, and Joan Waugh, eds. *The Memory of the Civil War in American Culture*. Chapel Hill: University of North Carolina Press, 2004.

Flood, Charles Bracelen. *Grant's Final Victory: Ulysses S. Grant's Heroic Last Year*. New York: DaCapo Press, 2011.

Foster, Gaines M. *Ghosts of the Confederacy: Defeat, the Lost Cause, and the Emergence of the New South*. Oxford, UK: Oxford University Press, 1987.

Franklin, John Hope. "A Century of Civil War Observance." *Journal of Negro History* 47, no. 2 (April 1962): 107.

Gallagher, Gary W. *Lee and His Generals in War and Memory*. Baton Rouge: Louisiana State University Press, 1998.

———. *Stephen Dodson Ramseur: Lee's Gallant General*. Chapel Hill: University of North Carolina Press, 1985.

———. *The Union War*. Cambridge, MA: Harvard University Press, 2011.

Gallagher, Gary W., and Alan T. Nolan, eds. *The Myth of the Lost Cause and Civil War History*. Bloomington: Indiana University Press, 2000.

Gannon, Barbara A. *The Won Cause: Black and White Comradeship in the Grand Army of the Republic*. Chapel Hill: University of North Carolina Press, 2011.

Garber, Wayne Edward, and Owen Early Harner. *The History of New Hope, Virginia*. Staunton, VA: Lot's Wife Publishing, 2006.

Garner, Stanton. *The Civil War World of Herman Melville*. Lawrence: University Press of Kansas, 1993.

Geier, Clarence, and Phoebe Hardin. *An Overview and Assessment of Cultural Resources and Landscapes within the Legislated Cedar Creek–Belle Grove National Historical Park*. Harrisonburg, VA: James Madison University, 2006.

Geier, Clarence, and Stephen R. Potter, eds. *Archaeological Perspectives on the American Civil War*. Gainesville: University Press of Florida, 2000.

Goldfield, David. *Still Fighting the Civil War: The American South and Southern History*. Baton Rouge: Louisiana State University Press, 2002.

Gold, Thomas Daniel. *History of Clarke County Virginia and Its Connection with the War Between the States*. Berryville, VA: C.R. Hughes, 1914.

Harris, M. Keith. *Across the Bloody Chasm: The Culture of Commemoration Among Civil War Veterans*. Baton Rouge: Louisiana State University Press, 2014.

Heatwole, John L. *The Burning: Sheridan in the Shenandoah Valley*. Charlottesville, VA: Rockbridge Publishing, 1998.

Bibliography

History of the Confederated Memorial Associations of the South. New Orleans: Graham Press, 1904.

History of the Easel Shaped Monument and a Key to the Principles and Objects of the Grand Army of the Republic and Its Co-Workers. Chicago: Dux Publishing Co., 1893.

History of the Ladies' Confederate Memorial Association: Winchester, Virginia. Winchester, VA: Farmers and Merchant National Bank, n.d.

Horton, R.G. *A Youth's History of the Great Civil War in the United States: From 1861–1865.* New York: Van Evrie, Horton, and Co., 1867.

Janney, Caroline E. *Burying the Dead But Not the Past: Ladies' Memorial Associations and the Lost Cause.* Chapel Hill: University of North Carolina Press, 2008.

——. *Remembering the Civil War: Reunion and the Limits of Reconciliation.* Chapel Hill: University of North Carolina Press, 2013.

Jones, Evan C., and Wiley Sword, eds. *Gateway to the Confederacy: New Perspectives on the Chickamauga and Chattanooga Campaigns, 1862–1863.* Baton Rouge: Louisiana University Press, 2014.

Jordan, Ervin L., Jr. *Black Confederates and Afro-Yankees in Civil War Virginia.* Charlottesville: University of Virginia Press, 1995.

Kinchen, Oscar A. *Women Who Spied for the Blue and Gray.* Philadelphia: Dorrance & Co., 1972.

Knight, Charles R. *Valley Thunder: The Battle of New Market and Opening of the Shenandoah Valley Campaign, May 1864.* New York: Savas Beatie, 2010.

Leekley, John, ed. *Bruce Catton: Reflections on the Civil War.* New York: Berkley Books, 1982.

Leiby, James. *Carroll Wright and Labor Reform: The Origin of Labor Statistics.* Cambridge, MA: Harvard University Press, 1960.

Logue, Larry M., and Michael Barton, eds. *The Civil War Veteran: A Historical Reader.* New York: New York University Press, 2007.

Mahon, Michael G. *The Shenandoah Valley: 1861–1865.* Mechanicsburg, PA: Stackpole Books, 1999.

Mallin, Robert, and Richard Radi. *Ashby Camp Revisited.* Winchester, VA: Robert Mallin and Richard C. Radi, 1995.

Marten, James M. *Sing Not War: The Lives of Union & Confederate Veterans in Gilded Age America.* Chapel Hill: University of North Carolina Press, 2011.

McClure, Alexander K., and Charles Morris. *The Authentic Life of William McKinley: Our Third Martyr President.* N.p.: W.E. Shull, 1901.

McConnell, Stuart M. *Glorious Contentment: The Grand Army of the Republic, 1865–1890.* Chapel Hill: University of North Carolina Press, 1992.

McPherson, James M. *This Mighty Scourge: Perspectives on the Civil War.* Oxford, UK: Oxford University Press, 2009.

Morton, Frederic. *The Story of Winchester in Virginia: The Oldest Town in the Shenandoah Valley.* Strasburg, VA: Shenandoah Publishing House, 1925.

Mountcastle, Clay. *Punitive War: Confederate Guerillas and Union Reprisals.* Lawrence: University Press of Kansas, 2009.

Neff, John R. *Honoring the Civil War Dead: Commemoration and the Problem of Reconciliation.* Lawrence: University Press of Kansas, 2005.

Nelson, Megan Kate. *Ruin Nation: Destruction and the American Civil War*. Athens: University of Georgia Press, 2012.

Noyalas, Jonathan A. *The Battle of Cedar Creek: Victory from the Jaws of Defeat*. Charleston, SC: The History Press, 2009.

———. *Plagued by War: Winchester, Virginia, During the Civil War*. Leesburg, VA: Gauley Mount Press, 2003.

———. *Stonewall Jackson's 1862 Valley Campaign: War Comes to the Homefront*. Charleston, SC: The History Press, 2010.

———. "'That Woman Was Worth a Whole Brigade.'" *Civil War Times* 51, no. 3 (June 2012): 43–49.

Patchan, Scott C. *The Last Battle of Winchester: Phil Sheridan, Jubal Early, and the Shenandoah Valley Campaign August 7–September 19, 1864*. El Dorado Hills, CA: Savas Beatie, 2013.

Phillips, Edward H. *The Lower Shenandoah Valley in the Civil War: Its Impact Upon the Civilian Populations and Upon Civilian Institutions*. Lynchburg, VA: H.E. Howard, 1993.

Pond, George E. *The Shenandoah Valley in 1864*. Edison, NJ: Castle Books, 2002.

Rable, George C. *God's Almost Chosen Peoples: A Religious History of the American Civil War*. Chapel Hill: University of North Carolina Press, 2010.

Robertson, James I., Jr. *Stonewall Jackson: The Man, The Soldier, The Legend*. New York: Macmillan, 1997.

Rogers, Phil S., ed. *Everlasting Glory: Vermont Soldiers Who Were Awarded the Congressional Medal of Honor for Service During the Civil War 1861–1865*. Hardwick, VT: Vermont Civil War Hemlocks, 2007.

Roland, Charles P. *History Teaches Us to Hope: Reflections on the Civil War and Southern History*. Lexington: University Press of Kentucky, 2010.

———. *Reflections on Lee: A Historian's Assessment*. Mechanicsburg, PA: Stackpole Books, 1995.

Samway, Patrick, ed. *Sign-Posts in a Strange Land: Walker Percy*. New York: Farrar, Straus, and Giroux, 1991.

Schildt, John W. *Charles Carleton Coffin: Eyewitness to Antietam*. Chewsville, MD: John W. Schildt, 2005.

Sedore, Timothy S. *An Illustrated Guide to Virginia's Confederate Monuments*. Carbondale: Southern Illinois University Press, 2011.

Sheehan-Dean, Aaron, ed. *A Companion to the U.S. Civil War*. 2 vols. Malden, MA: Wiley-Blackwell, 2014.

Shenandoah Valley Battlefields Foundation. *Shenandoah Valley Battlefields National Historic District: Final Management Plan*. New Market, VA: Shenandoah Valley Battlefields Foundation, 2000.

Silber, Nina. *The Romance of Reunion: Northerners and the South, 1865–1900*. Chapel Hill: University of North Carolina Press, 1993.

Smith, Timothy B. *A Chickamauga Memorial: The Establishment of America's First Civil War National Military Park*. Knoxville: University of Tennessee Press, 2009.

Starr, Stephen Z. *The Union Cavalry in the Civil War: The War in the East, From Gettysburg to Appomattox, 1863–1865*. Baton Rouge: Louisiana State University Press, 2007.

BIBLIOGRAPHY

Steele, Joel Dorman, and Esther Baker Steele. *A Brief History of the United States*. New York: American Book Company, 1885.

Sutton, Robert K., ed. *Rally on the High Ground: The National Park Service Symposium on the Civil War*. Fort Washington, PA: Eastern National, 2001.

Swinton, William. *Campaigns of the Army of the Potomac*. Secaucus, NJ: Blue & Grey Press, 1988.

Toomey, Daniel Carroll. *Hero at Front Royal: The Life of General John R. Kenly*. Baltimore, MD: Toomey Press, 2009.

United States Treasury Register: Containing a List of All Persons Employed in the Treasury Department. Washington, D.C.: Government Printing Office, 1873.

Varon, Elizabeth R. *Appomattox: Victory, Defeat, and Freedom at the End of the Civil War*. Oxford, UK: Oxford University Press, 2014.

Waugh, Joan. *U.S. Grant: American Hero, American Myth*. Chapel Hill: University of North Carolina Press, 2009.

Waugh, Joan, and Gary W. Gallagher, eds. *Wars Within a War: Controversy and Conflict Over the American Civil War*. Chapel Hill: University of North Carolina Press, 2009.

Wayland, John W. *A History of Rockingham County, Virginia*. Dayton, VA: Ruebush-Elkins Co., 1912.

Webb, Willard, ed. *Crucial Moments of the Civil War*. New York: Bonanza Books, 1961.

Wert, Jeffry D. *From Winchester to Cedar Creek: The Shenandoah Campaign of 1864*. Mechanicsburg, PA: Stackpole Books, 1997.

DISSERTATIONS

Berkey, Jonathan M. "War in the Borderland: The Civilians' Civil War in Virginia's Lower Shenandoah Valley." PhD diss., Pennsylvania State University, 2003.

INDEX

About the Author

J onathan A. Noyalas is assistant
professor of history and director
of the Center for Civil War History
at Lord Fairfax Community
College in Middletown, Virginia.
He has also served twice as the
Hugh and Virginia McCormick
visiting chair in Civil War History
at Shenandoah University in
Winchester. The author or editor
of eleven books on Civil War–era
history, Professor Noyalas has also
authored scores of articles, reviews,
essays and book chapters for a
variety of publications, including
Civil War Times, *America's Civil War*,
Civil War Monitor, *Blue & Gray*,
Hallowed Ground and *Civil War News*.
Additionally, Professor Noyalas has
served as a historian and consultant
for a variety of public history
projects, including the National
Park Service's historic resource

Photograph by Brandy Noyalas.

study at Cedar Creek and Belle Grove National Historical Park (Civil War historian), the Civil War Trust's Cedar Creek Battle App (content expert) and *National Geographic*'s three-part documentary series "Civil Warriors," which debuted in the United States in April 2012 (consultant). He has also appeared on C-SPAN's American History TV. Active in battlefield preservation in the Shenandoah Valley, Professor Noyalas is the past chair and current member of the Shenandoah Valley Battlefields Foundation's committee on interpretation and education.

Visit us at
www.historypress.net
....
This title is also available as an e-book

www.ingramcontent.com/pod-product-compliance
Lightning Source LLC
Chambersburg PA
CBHW060758100426
42813CB00004B/865